BIRDS
of
DENVER
and the
FRONT RANGE

D0034119

Chris C. Fisher
Greg Butcher

LONE
PINE

The Publisher: Lone Pine Publishing

1901 Raymond Ave. SW, Ste. C	206, 10426 – 81 Ave.	202A, 1110 Seymour St.
Renton, WA 98055	Edmonton, AB T6E 1X5	Vancouver, BC V6B 3N3
USA	Canada	Canada

Canadian Cataloguing in Publication Data

Fisher, Chris C. (Christopher Charles)
    Birds of Denver and the Front Range

    Includes bibliographical references and index.
    ISBN 1-55105-106-0

    1. Birds—Colorado—Denver—Identification. 2. Bird watching—Colorado—Denver. I. Butcher, Greg, 1952–
II. Title.

QL684.C6F57 1997   598'.09788'83   C97-910646-X

Senior Editor: Nancy Foulds
Project Editor: Roland Lines
Technical Review: Wayne Campbell
Production Manager: David Dodge
Production and Layout: Michelle Bynoe
Book Design: Carol S. Dragich
Cover Design: Jun Lee
Cover Illustration: Gary Ross
Map: Volker Bodegom
Illustrations: Gary Ross, Ted Nordhagen, Ewa Pluciennik, Horst Krause
Separations and Film: Elite Lithographers Co. Ltd., Edmonton, Alberta, Canada
Printing: Quality Colour Press Inc., Edmonton, Alberta, Canada

The publisher gratefully acknowledges the assistance of the Department of Canadian Heritage and Alberta Community Development, and the financial support provided by the Alberta Foundation for the Arts.

Contents

Acknowledgments

A book such as this is made possible by the inspired work of Denver's naturalist community, whose contributions continue to advance the science of ornithology and to motivate a new generation of nature lovers.

My thanks go to Gary Ross and Ted Nordhagen, whose illustrations have elevated the quality of this book; to Carole Patterson, for her continual support; to the birding societies of the Denver area, which all make daily contributions to natural history; to Lisa Takats and Gord Court for their input; to the team at Lone Pine Publishing—Roland Lines, Nancy Foulds, Eloise Pulos, Greg Brown, Michelle Bynoe and Shane Kennedy—for their input and steering; to John Acorn and Jim Butler, for their stewardship and their remarkable passion; and, finally, to Wayne Campbell, a premier naturalist whose works have served as models of excellence, for his thorough and helpful review of the text.

Chris C. Fisher

Introduction

No matter where we live, birds are a natural part of our lives. We are so used to seeing them that we often take their presence for granted. When we take the time to notice their colors, songs and behaviors, we experience their dynamic appeal.

This book presents a brief introduction into the lives of birds. It is intended to serve as both a bird identification guide and a bird appreciation guide. Getting to know the names of birds is the first step toward getting to know birds. Once we've made contact with a species, we can better appreciate its character and mannerisms during future encounters. Over a lifetime of meetings, many birds become acquaintances, some seen daily, others not for years.

The selection of 125 bird species described in this book represents a balance between the familiar and the noteworthy: many are the most common species found in the Denver area; some are less common, but they are noteworthy because they are important ecologically or because their particular status grants them a high profile. It would be impossible for a beginners' book such as this to comprehensively describe all the birds found in the Denver area. Furthermore, there is no one site where all the species within this book can be observed simultaneously, but most species can be viewed—at least seasonally—within a short drive from Denver.

It is hoped that this guide will inspire novice birdwatchers into spending some time outdoors, gaining valuable experience with the local bird community. This book stresses the identity of birds, but it also attempts to bring them to life by discussing their various character traits. We often discuss these traits in human terms, because personifying a bird's character can help us to feel a bond with the birds. The perceived links with birds should not be mistaken for actual behaviors, however, because our interpretations can falsely reflect the complexities of bird life.

FEATURES OF THE LANDSCAPE

Rising from the Great Plains at the base of the Rocky Mountains, the city of Denver is within reach of a uniquely diverse environment that is home to one of the richest collections of birdlife in the country. The Denver area is where east and west converge: the rolling plains to the east are home to a wide range of Great Plains species; to the west, the imposing mountains are home to a distinctly western variety of birdlife. Denver also lies within a north-south bird migration path known as the Central Flyway. A wide variety of species pass along this corridor as they follow the mountains north or south, and Colorado boasts one of the largest species lists in the country. The distribution of birdlife in the Denver area is significantly influenced by seasonality and habitat. Many species of birds that are common at higher elevations are rarely found near the city limits.

The Denver area's mountain parks are highly sought after by birders. Genesee Mountain Park, one of the area's largest parks, is easily spotted from the city, and it may be reached within an afternoon's travel. High in the foothills, scattered patches of trembling aspen grow amid the more common stands of blue spruce, Douglas-fir and ponderosa pine. These aspen groves stand out from the coniferous communities of these mountain sides and are especially rich in species diversity. Another uniquely beautiful area west of Denver is Red Rocks Park. Home to a different variety of birdlife, its spectacular cliffs loom conspicuously amid the pinyon pines and juniper trees of the foothills.

The landscape immediately around Denver is largely short-grass prairie and agricultural land. Great numbers of birds can be found in the small portions of original grassland that remain, but the more common agricultural fields are suitable for a smaller variety of prairie species. At most times of the year, the fence-lined fields of Denver's countryside are a favorite spot for many hawks. Rocky Mountain Arsenal, a wildlife refuge for many prairie species, offers unique year-round opportunities for the avid birder. Among the pockets of trees and overgrown fields, expect to find magpies, sparrows, blackbirds and many species of raptors. During the summer months, these areas provide nesting sites for many species, and, with help from the prairie dog population, endangered Burrowing Owls can be found perched alongside their nesting burrows.

Artificial reservoirs are common near Denver's arid plains, where naturally flowing water is a scarce commodity, and they attract seasonal

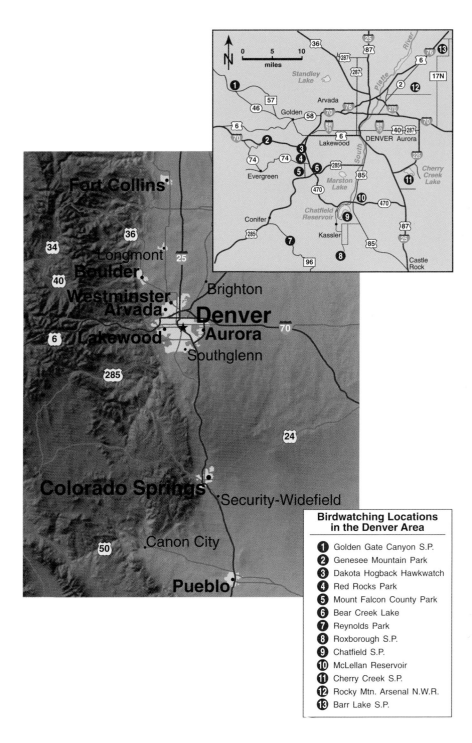

Birdwatching Locations in the Denver Area

1. Golden Gate Canyon S.P.
2. Genesee Mountain Park
3. Dakota Hogback Hawkwatch
4. Red Rocks Park
5. Mount Falcon County Park
6. Bear Creek Lake
7. Reynolds Park
8. Roxborough S.P.
9. Chatfield S.P.
10. McLellan Reservoir
11. Cherry Creek S.P.
12. Rocky Mtn. Arsenal N.W.R.
13. Barr Lake S.P.

concentrations of loons, grebes, ducks, gulls and terns. Areas such as the Prospect Reservoir and Cherry Creek State Park provide a reliable source of water for many species. During the summer months, the drainage of water for irrigation purposes exposes the underlying mudflats, making these areas particularly alluring to many shorebirds, gulls, grebes and other waterbirds. Just a few miles from Denver's city limits, the prairie lakes and shallow marshes of the Barr Lake drainage feature an impressive abundance of shorebirds, grebes, rails and waterfowl.

Flowing through the heart of Denver, the South Platte River and its tributaries provide favorable habitat for many resident and migratory species. These riparian areas, such as at Chatfield State Park, are very productive habitats for viewing species that otherwise might pass through Denver undetected. West of the city, where the slopes of the Great Plains rise to form the foothills, local canyons and valleys are lined with lush willow and cottonwood communities, each with their own birding flavor.

Denver's city parks and backyards also attract birdlife. Early settlers to this area established a system of city parks that now attracts a great diversity of species. Many of the birds you will find in the Denver area are accustomed to humans and tolerate our intrusions into their lives, and landscaped settings are often among the best places to become familiar with birdlife. Backyard feeders are a welcome invitation throughout Denver's unpredictable winters. During the warmer months, many birds make use of backyard nest boxes, delighting area residents. Even in the city's most modified areas, you will easily find large numbers of pigeons, sparrows and starlings, and even a few unexpected specialists, such as the Peregrine Falcon.

THE IMPORTANCE OF HABITAT

Understanding the relationship between habitat and bird species often helps identify which birds are which. Because you won't find a loon up a tree or a quail out at sea, habitat is an important thing to note when birdwatching.

The quality of habitat is one of the most powerful factors to influence bird distribution. With experience you may become amazed by the predictability of some birds within a specific habitat type. The habitat icons in this book show where each species can most commonly be found. It is important to realize, however, that because of their migratory habits, birds are sometimes found in completely different habitats.

Habitat Icons

Each bird in this guide is accompanied by at least one habitat symbol, which represents a general environment where the bird is most likely to be seen. Most birds will be seen in one of their associated habitats, but migrants can turn up in just about any habitat type. These unexpected surprises (despite being confusing to novice birders) are among the most powerful motivations for the increasing legion of birdwatchers.

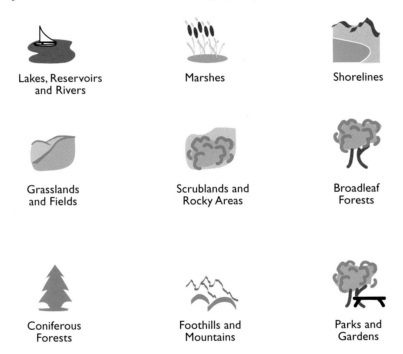

Lakes, Reservoirs
and Rivers

Marshes

Shorelines

Grasslands
and Fields

Scrublands and
Rocky Areas

Broadleaf
Forests

Coniferous
Forests

Foothills and
Mountains

Parks and
Gardens

THE ORGANIZATION OF THIS BOOK

To simplify field identification, *Birds of Denver and the Front Range* is organized slightly differently from many other field guides that use strict phylogenetic groupings. In cases where many birds from the same family are described, conventional groupings are maintained. In other cases, however, distantly related birds that share physical and behavioral similarities are grouped together. This blend of family grouping and physically similar supergroups strives to help the novice birdwatcher identify and appreciate the birds he or she encounters.

DIVING BIRDS

loons, grebes, pelicans, cormorants

These heavy-bodied birds are adapted to diving for their food. Between their underwater foraging dives, they are most frequently seen on the surface of the water. These birds could only be confused with one another or with certain diving ducks.

WETLAND WADERS

herons, ibises, soras, coots

Although this group varies considerably in size, and represents three separate families of birds, wetland waders share similar habitat and food preferences. Some of these long-legged birds of marshes are quite common, but certain species are heard far more than they are seen.

WATERFOWL

geese, ducks

Waterfowl tend to have stout bodies and webbed feet, and they are swift in flight. Although most species are associated with water, waterfowl can sometimes be seen grazing on upland sites.

VULTURES, HAWKS AND FALCONS

vultures, eagles, hawks, falcons

From deep forests to open country to large lakes, there are hawks and falcons hunting the skies. Their predatory look—with sharp talons, hooked bills and forward-facing eyes—easily identifies this group. Hawks generally forage during the day, and many use their broad wings to soar in thermals and updrafts.

GAMEBIRDS

pheasants, grouse, turkeys

These birds bear a superficial resemblance to chickens. They are stout birds and poor flyers, and they are most often encountered on the ground or when flushed.

SHOREBIRDS

killdeers, sandpipers, phalaropes etc.

Although these small, long-legged, swift-flying birds are mainly found along the shores, don't be surprised to find certain species in pastures and marshy areas.

GULLS AND TERNS

Gulls are relatively large, usually light-colored birds that are frequently seen swimming, walking about in urban areas or soaring gracefully over the city. Their backs tend to be darker than their bellies, and their feet are webbed. Terns are not often seen on the ground, they rarely soar, and they have straight, pointed bills.

DOVES

Denver's doves are easily recognizable. Rock Doves are found in all urban areas, from city parks to the downtown core. These urban doves have many of the same physical and behavioral characteristics as the 'wilder' Mourning Doves.

NOCTURNAL BIRDS

owls, nighthawks

These night hunters have large eyes. Owls, which primarily prey on rodents, have powerful, taloned feet and strongly hooked bills. Nighthawks catch moths and other nocturnal insects on the wing. Although owls are primarily active at night, their distinctive calls enable bird-watchers to readily identify them.

KINGFISHERS

The kingfisher's behavior and physical characteristics are quite unlike any bird in Denver. It primarily hunts fish, plunging after them from the air or from an overhanging perch.

WOODPECKERS

The drumming sound of hammering wood and their precarious foraging habits easily identify most woodpeckers. They are frequently seen in forests, clinging to trunks and chipping away bark with their straight, sturdy bills. Even when these birds cannot be seen or heard, the characteristic marks of certain species can be seen on trees in any mature forest.

HUMMINGBIRDS

Hummingbirds are Denver's smallest birds, and their bright colors and swift flight are very characteristic.

FLYCATCHERS

flycatchers, phoebes, kingbirds, etc.

As their name implies, flycatchers catch insects on the wing, darting after them from a favorite perch. Most flycatchers sing simple but distinctive songs. Many flycatchers have subdued plumage, but phoebes and kingbirds are rather colorful.

SWIFTS AND SWALLOWS

Members of these two families are typically seen at their nest sites or in flight. Small but sleek, swifts and swallows have narrow wings and short tails, and they are nearly always seen in flight. Although swallows are superficially similar to swifts in behavior and appearance, the two groups are not closely related.

JAYS AND CROWS

jays, magpies, crows, ravens

Many members of this family are known for their intelligence and adaptability. They are easily observed birds that are frequently extremely bold, teasing the animal-human barrier. They are sometimes called 'corvids,' from Corvidae, the scientific name for the family.

SMALL SONGBIRDS

chickadees, nuthatches, wrens, etc.

Birds in this group are all generally smaller than a sparrow. Many of them associate with one another in mixed-species flocks. Most are commonly encountered in city parks, backyards and other wooded areas.

BLUEBIRDS AND THRUSHES

bluebirds, solitaires, thrushes, robins

From the robin to the secretive forest thrushes, this group of beautiful singers has the finest collective voice. Although some thrushes are very familiar, others require a little experience and patience to identify.

VIREOS AND WARBLERS

vireos, warblers, yellowthroats, chats

Warblers are splashed liberally with colors, while vireos tend to dress in pale olive. These birds are all very small and sing characteristic courtship songs.

MID-SIZED SONGBIRDS

tanagers, starlings, waxwings, etc.

The birds within this group are all sized between a sparrow and a robin. Waxwings are reserved in dress and voice, and starlings are frequently seen and heard all over the Denver area.

SPARROWS

towhees, sparrows, juncos

These small, often indistinct birds are predominantly brown. Their songs are often very useful in identification. Many birdwatchers discount many of these sparrows as simply 'little brown birds'—the towhees and Lark Bunting are colorful exceptions—which is unfortunate, because these birds are worthy of the extra identification effort.

BLACKBIRDS AND ORIOLES

blackbirds, cowbirds, orioles, etc.

Most of these birds are predominantly black and have relatively long tails. They are common in open areas, city parks and agricultural fields. Western Meadowlarks belong in the blackbird family despite not being black and having short tails.

FINCH-LIKE BIRDS

finches, grosbeaks, buntings, etc.

These finches and finch-like birds are primarily adapted to feeding on seeds, and they have stout, conical bills. Many are birdfeeder regulars, and they are a familiar part of the winter scene.

ABUNDANCE CHARTS

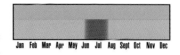

Accompanying each bird description is a chart that indicates the relative abundance of the species throughout the year. These stylized graphs offer some insight into the distribution and abundance of the birds, but they should not be viewed as definitive; they represent a generalized overview. There may be inconsistencies specific to time and location, but these charts should provide readers with a basic reference for bird abundance and occurrence.

Each chart is divided into the 12 months of the year. The pale orange that colors the chart is an indication of abundance: the higher the color, the more common the bird. Dark orange is used to indicate the nesting period. The time frame of breeding is approximate, and nesting birds can certainly be found both before and after the period indicated on the chart. Where no nesting color is shown, the bird breeds outside the area—mainly to the north and east—and visits Denver in significant numbers during migration or in winter.

These graphs are based on personal observations and on *A Birder's Guide to Colorado* (Holt 1997).

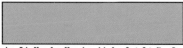

Jan Feb Mar Apr May Jun Jul Aug Sept Oct Nov Dec
abundant

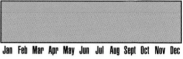

Jan Feb Mar Apr May Jun Jul Aug Sept Oct Nov Dec
common

Jan Feb Mar Apr May Jun Jul Aug Sept Oct Nov Dec
uncommon

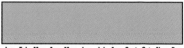

Jan Feb Mar Apr May Jun Jul Aug Sept Oct Nov Dec
rare

Jan Feb Mar Apr May Jun Jul Aug Sept Oct Nov Dec
unlikely

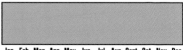

Jan Feb Mar Apr May Jun Jul Aug Sept Oct Nov Dec
absent

BIRDS
of
DENVER
and the FRONT RANGE

Common Loon
Gavia immer

The Common Loon is a noble symbol of northern wilderness, preferring the diminishing pristine areas where birds alone quarrel over naval rights-of-way. Loons no longer breed in our area, but they visit each year during migration and in winter. Although their intricate dark green and white breeding wardrobe has given way to winter browns, it is in fall that these birds can best be seen gingerly floating in the waters on McClellan Reservoir.

Loons routinely poke their heads underwater to look for potential prey and plot their forthcoming pursuit. They dive deeply and efficiently, compressing their feathers to reduce underwater drag and to decrease their buoyancy. Propelling themselves primarily with their legs, these birds can outswim fish over short distances. Because they have solid bones (unlike chickens and most other birds, which have hollow bones) and because their legs are placed well back on their bodies for diving, Common Loons require long stretches of open water for take-off. Every year, some loons are fatally trapped by constricting ice as lakes freeze in fall.

Similar Species: Common Merganser (p. 38) has an orange bill and very white plumage. Double-crested Cormorant (p. 22) has all-black plumage and a long neck, and it usually holds its bill pointed upward when it swims.

non-breeding

Quick I.D.: larger than a duck; sexes similar; stout, sharp bill. *In flight:* hunchbacked. *Breeding:* dark green hood; black and white checkerboard back; fine, white 'necklace.' *Non-breeding:* sandy-brown back; light underparts.
Size: 27–33 in.

Jan Feb Mar Apr May Jun Jul Aug Sept Oct Nov Dec

Eared Grebe
Podiceps nigricollis

Eared Grebes are common in shallow marshes and lakes from March to November. They are commonly seen on McClellan Reservoir and Standley Lake during migration, and usually a small colony establishes its flotilla of nests in calm waters. Grebes are among the purest of waterbirds, even their nests are not far from water: they float upon the water's surface, leaving their eggy contents bathed in a shallow pool of water. This pre-birth introduction to water is consistent with the remainder of the bird's life, finding all that it requires in headfirst dives under the water.

All grebes eat feathers, a seemingly strange habit that frequently causes their digestive systems to become packed. It is thought that this behavior may protect their stomachs from sharp fish bones, and it may also slow the passage of food through the digestive system so that more nutrients can be absorbed. The toes of grebes are also unusual: unlike the fully webbed feet of ducks, gulls and cormorants, grebes' toes are individually lobed.

Similar Species: Horned Grebe is the same size and has a red neck in the breeding season and a bolder white face patch in the non-breeding season. Pied-billed Grebe has dark underparts, lacks the golden ear tufts in the breeding season and has a yellow bill and dark eyes in the non-breeding season.

breeding

Quick I.D.: smaller than a duck; sexes similar. *Breeding:* golden ear tufts; black neck, back and head; white underparts; short bill (shorter than width of head); red eyes. *Non-breeding:* small white patch behind ear.
Size: 12¹/₂–15 in.

Jan Feb Mar Apr May Jun Jul Aug Sept Oct Nov Dec

Western Grebe
Aechmophorus occidentalis

The courtship display of the Western Grebe is one of the most elaborate breeding rituals of North American wildlife. During the 'weed dance,' the male and female both raise their torsos gently out of the water, caressing each other with aquatic vegetation held in their long, rapier-like bills. The pair's bond is fully reinforced by the 'rushing' phase, during which the birds glance at one another before exploding into a sprint across the water's surface. Both grebes stand high, their wings held back and their heads and necks rigid, until the race ends with the pair breaking the water's surface in a headfirst dive. By following your eyes and ears at Standley Lake or Barr Lake in May, this marvel can be witnessed first-hand. The performance peaks at dawn and dusk, and it is not uncommon to continue to hear the dancing birds long after the failing light of dusk has dimmed the spectacle from view.

Similar Species: Double-crested Cormorant (p. 22) lacks the clean white underparts. Common Loon (p. 18) has a shorter, stocky neck. Eared Grebe (p. 19) is much smaller. Clark's Grebe has white around the eyes and an orange-yellow bill, and it is often found with Western Grebes.

Jan Feb Mar Apr May Jun Jul Aug Sept Oct Nov Dec

Quick I.D.: larger than a duck; sexes similar; long, slender neck; black upper-parts, from base of bill to tail; white underparts, from chin through belly; long, thin, yellow bill; white lower cheek; red eyes.
Size: 20–24 in.

American White Pelican
Pelecanus erythrorhynchos

non-breeding

With a wingspan unsurpassed by any other Rocky Mountain bird, the purposeful and confident flight of the American White Pelican is an unforgettable experience. American White Pelicans are one of the easiest of North American birds to identify, and it is quite a luxury for Denver-area residents to have them at West Quincy Lakes and Barr Lake for most of the warmer months. In flight, pelicans are often seen skimming low over lakes: their bellies pass just over the waves as the birds use the subtle air currents rising from the water's surface to help them glide.

Group foraging is a rare activity among birds, and it is often used as evidence to highlight this bird's impressive social relations. Flocks of swimming white pelicans circle and herd fish, scooping up the prey with careful dips of their large bills.

Similar Species: Snow Goose is smaller and has a much smaller bill. Tundra Swan lacks the black wing tips and has a longer, thinner neck.

Quick I.D.: swan-sized; sexes similar; stocky, white bird; long, orange bill and throat pouch; black primary and secondary wing feathers; short tail; naked orange skin patch around eye. *Breeding*: small, keeled plate develops on upper mandible; pale yellow crest on back of head. *Non-breeding* and *Immature*: white plumage is tinged with gray.
Size: 54–70 in.

Jan Feb Mar Apr May Jun Jul Aug Sept Oct Nov Dec

Double-crested Cormorant
Phalacrocorax auritus

When Double-crested Cormorants are seen flying in single-file, low over McClelland Reservoir, the prehistoric sight hints to their ancestry. The tight, dark flocks soar and sail over lakes, until hunger or the need for rest draws them to the water's surface. It is there that cormorants are most comfortable, disappearing beneath the surface in deep foraging dives.

Cormorants lack the ability to waterproof their feathers, so they need to dry their wings after each swim. They are frequently seen perched on bridge pilings and beached logs with their wings partially spread to expose their wet feathers to the sun and wind. It would seem to be a great disadvantage for a waterbird to have to dry its wings, but the cormorant's ability to wet its feathers decreases the bird's buoyancy, making it easier for the cormorant to swim after the fish on which it preys. Sealed nostrils, a long, rudder-like tail and excellent underwater vision are other features of the cormorant's aquatic lifestyle.

Similar Species: Common Loon (p. 18) has a shorter neck and is more stout overall. Mergansers (p. 38) are smaller and not as dark.

breeding

Quick I.D.: goose-sized; sexes similar; all-black plumage; long tail; long neck. *In flight:* kinked neck; rapid wing beats. *Breeding:* bright orange throat pouch; black or white plumes streaming back from eyebrows (seen only at close range). *First-year:* brown; pale neck, breast and belly.
Size: 30–35 in.

Jan Feb Mar Apr May Jun Jul Aug Sept Oct Nov Dec

Great Blue Heron
Ardea herodias

breeding

The Great Blue Heron is one of the largest and most regal of the birds in our area. It often stands motionless as it surveys the calm waters, its graceful lines blending naturally with the grasses and cattails of wetlands. All herons have specialized vertebrae that enable the neck to fold back over itself. The S-shaped neck, seen in flight, identifies all members of this wading family.

Hunting herons space themselves out evenly in favorite hunting spots, and they will strike out suddenly at prey below the water's surface. In flight, their lazy wing beats slowly but effortlessly carry them up to their nests. These herons nest communally high in trees, building bulky stick nests that are in plain site at Chatfield State Park and other regional wetlands. The shallows of Barr Lake and South Platte Park produce good views of this common summer and uncommon winter bird.

Similar Species: Black-crowned Night-Heron (p. 24) is smaller.

Quick I.D.: very large heron; eagle-sized wingspan; sexes similar; gray-blue plumage; long legs; long, dagger-like, yellow bill; red thighs. *In flight:* head folded back; legs held straight back.
Size: 48–52 in.

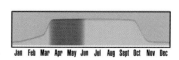

Jan Feb Mar Apr May Jun Jul Aug Sept Oct Nov Dec

Black-crowned Night-Heron
Nycticorax nycticorax

As daylight fades, a distinctive *wok-wok* call announces a flock of Black-crowned Night-Herons flying to a marsh. It is at this time of day that these birds prefer to feed, and their shapes can be among the last forms visible in summer's golden evening light. These pony-tailed birds possess remarkably large eyes, a possible advantage in their nocturnal foraging efforts.

Black-crowned Night-Herons are much more difficult to find in the middle of the day, because they roost inconspicuously in shoreline vegetation. They nest in low bushes, and have generally become increasingly uncommon in our area in the past decades. The degradation and destruction of vital wetlands have resulted in a sharp decline in this bird's abundance. Black-crowned Night-Herons can still occasionally be spotted skulking in the twilight hours along the shores of Barr Lake, South Platte Park and other areas that have maintained wetlands in their natural state.

Similar Species: Great Blue Heron (p. 23) is larger and has a long neck. Green Heron has a greenish-black cap, a chestnut neck and greenish upperparts. American Bittern is similar to a juvenile night-heron, but it has black wing tips and a black mustache stripe.

Quick I.D.: mid-sized heron; sexes similar; black crown and back; gray neck and wings; white cheek and belly; moderately long legs. *Breeding:* white plumes from back of head. *Juvenile:* brown; heavily streaked and spotted.
Size: 24–26 in.

Jan Feb Mar Apr May Jun Jul Aug Sept Oct Nov Dec

White-faced Ibis
Plegadis chihi

breeding

In the shallows of Barr Lake, White-faced Ibises can regularly be seen rooting around in the soft bottoms with their long bills. During summer, these birds are generally seen standing in ankle-deep water, their bills allowing them to probe deeply into the animal-rich muddy substrate.

These long-legged birds are famous for their wanderings. When conditions are favorable for breeding, these strong flyers can miraculously arrive and nest in an area that historically has been unsuitable. Similarly, during fall, their post-breeding wanderings carry them far afield, and with its growing population, the White-faced Ibis can be increasingly expected at Denver-area wetlands and marshes.

Similar Species: Long-billed Curlew has a light brown body and a daintier bill. Herons (pp. 23–24) and egrets lack the thick, downcurved bill.

Quick I.D.: smaller than a heron; sexes similar; dark chestnut plumage; long, downcurved bill; long, dark legs; white feathers bordering naked facial patch; greenish lower back and wing covers; dark red eyes. *In flight:* outstretched neck. *Breeding:* rich red legs and facial patch.
Size: 19–26 in.

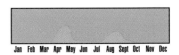

Jan Feb Mar Apr May Jun Jul Aug Sept Oct Nov Dec

Sora
Porzana carolina

Skulking around freshwater marshes in the Denver area is the seldom-seen Sora. Although this rail arrives in good numbers in spring, it is not a species that can be encountered with any predictability. Visual meetings with the Sora in Denver arise unexpectedly, usually when birdwatchers are out in a wetland searching for less reclusive species. Although the Sora's numbers have declined in our area, its loud call, *So-ra, So-ra,* followed by a descending whinny, can still be heard at many area marshes.

Urban sprawl and agricultural expansion have come at the expense of many Denver birds. The Sora's marshland habitat is often thought to be unproductive by human standards, but these shallow, nutrient-rich wetlands host a bounty of wildlife. With the growing legion of birdwatchers and nature lovers, societal values are finally shifting toward a holistic understanding of our natural communities.

Similar Species: Virginia Rail has a long, reddish, downcurved bill.

breeding

Jan Feb Mar Apr May Jun Jul Aug Sept Oct Nov Dec

Quick I.D.: robin-sized; sexes similar; short, yellow bill; front of face is black; gray neck and breast; long, greenish legs.
Size: 8–10 in.

American Coot
Fulica americana

The American Coot is a curious mix of comedy and confusion: it seems to have been made up of bits and pieces leftover from other birds. It has the lobed toes of a grebe, the bill of a chicken and the body shape and swimming habits of a duck, but it is not remotely related to any of these species: its closest cousins are rails and cranes. American Coots dabble and dive in water and forage on land, and they eat both plant and animal matter. They can be found in just about every freshwater pond, lake, marsh, lagoon or city park in Denver.

These loud, grouchy birds are seen chugging along in wetlands, frequently entering into short-lived disputes with other coots. American Coots appear comical while they swim: their heads bob in time with their paddling feet, and as a coot's swimming speed increases, so does the back-and-forth motion of its head. At peak speed, this motion seems to disorient the coot, so it prefers to run, flap and splash to the other side of the wetland.

Similar Species: All ducks (pp. 29–39) and grebes (pp. 19–20) generally lack the uniform black color and the white bill.

Quick I.D.: smaller than a duck; sexes similar; black body; white bill; red forehead shield; short tail; long legs; lobed feet; white undertail coverts.
Size: 14–16 in.

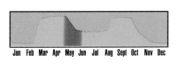

Jan Feb Mar Apr May Jun Jul Aug Sept Oct Nov Dec

Canada Goose
Branta canadensis

Most flocks of Canada Geese in city parks and golf courses show little concern for their human neighbors. These urban geese seem to think nothing of creating a traffic jam, blocking a fairway or dining on lawns. Their love of manicured parks and gardens and the lack of predators have created somewhat of a population explosion in parts of the Denver area.

Breeding pairs of Canada Geese are regal in appearance and their loyalty is legendary. They mate for life, and it's common for a mate to stay at the side of a fallen partner. Canada Geese are common along the shore of South Platte Park, West Quincy Lakes and Barr Lake during every season of the year.

Similar Species: None.

Jan Feb Mar Apr May Jun Jul Aug Sept Oct Nov Dec

Quick I.D.: large goose; sexes similar; white cheek; black head and neck; brown body; white undertail coverts.
Size: 35–42 in.

American Wigeon
Anas americana

Flocks of wigeons waddle across lawns in South Platte Park, grazing on the green grass. The white top and gray sides of the male American Wigeon's head look somewhat like a balding scalp, while the nasal spring calls, *wee-he-he-he*, sound remarkably like the squeaks of a squeezed rubber ducky.

Although they breed in our area, American Wigeons become more visible during their migratory passages. During spring and fall, American Wigeons can easily be found and identified in the shallows and grassy shorelines of Denver's ponds. The concentrated spring run north is generally less productive for birdwatchers than the return of the birds through the month of October. From this time until their spring movement, American Wigeon are among the most common and easily seen ducks, huddling around open waterbodies during the coldest weather.

Similar Species: Green-winged Teal is smaller and has a white shoulder slash and a rusty head with a green swipe. Gadwall is grayer and larger.

Quick I.D.: mid-sized duck; cinnamon breast and flanks; white belly; gray bill with black tip; green speculum. *Male:* white forehead; green swipe running back from each eye. *Female:* lacks distinct color on head.
Size: 18–21 in.

Jan Feb Mar Apr May Jun Jul Aug Sept Oct Nov Dec

Mallard
Anas platyrhynchos

The Mallard is the classic duck of inland marshes—the male's iridescent green head and chestnut breast are symbolic of wetland habitat. This large duck is commonly seen feeding in city parks, small lakes and shallow bays. With their legs positioned under the middle part of their bodies, Mallards walk easily, and they can spring straight out of water without a running start.

The Mallard is the most common duck in North America (and the Northern Hemisphere), and it is easily seen year-round in Denver. During winter, flocks of Mallards are seen in open water or grazing along shorelines. Because several duck species often band together in these loose flocks, birdwatchers habitually scan these groups to test their identification skills. Male Mallards have an 'eclipse' plumage during part of the year; at that time, they look like females.

Similar Species: Female resembles many other female dabbling ducks (pp. 29–34), but look for the blue speculum bordered by white on both sides and her close association with the male. Male Northern Shoveler (p. 33) has a green head, a white breast and chestnut flanks.

Jan Feb Mar Apr May Jun Jul Aug Sept Oct Nov Dec

Quick I.D.: large duck; bright orange feet; blue speculum bordered by white. *Male:* iridescent green head; yellow bill; chestnut breast; grayish flanks. *Female:* mottled brown; orange bill marked with black. **Size:** 22–26 in.

Blue-winged Teal
Anas discors

The male Blue-winged Teal has a thin, white crescent on his cheek and a steel-blue head to match his inner wing patches. These small ducks are extremely swift flyers, which frustrates their many predators. Their sleek design and rapid wing beats enable teals to swerve, even at great speeds, and also give these small ducks the accuracy to make pinpoint landings.

Unlike many of the larger dabblers, which overwinter in the United States, most teals migrate to Central and South America. For this reason, the Blue-winged Teal is often the last duck to arrive in Denver during spring and the first to leave in fall, usually by the end of September. During their vital time spent in our area, May is the most productive time to view them. During a walk around the fine lakeside trail system in Barr Lake State Park, these colorful ducks will certainly be encountered by observant visitors.

Similar Species: Female is easily confused with other female ducks.

Quick I.D.: small duck; blue forewing; green speculum; gray bill; yellow-orange legs. *Male:* steel-blue head; white crescent on cheek. *Female:* small, plain.
Size: 14–16 in.

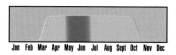

Jan Feb Mar Apr May Jun Jul Aug Sept Oct Nov Dec

Cinnamon Teal
Anas cyanoptera

When the morning sun strikes a spring wetland, the male Cinnamon Teal glows upon the waters like embers. These handsome ducks are frequently seen swimming along the surface of wetlands, their heads partially submerged, skimming aquatic invertebrates and small seeds from the pond's surface. Often, a series of ducks can be seen following a foraging leader, taking advantage of the sediments the front duck stirs up in the shallows with its paddling feet.

Cinnamon Teals are one of the many species of ducks that commonly nest in Colorado. In a concealed hollow in tall vegetation, occasionally far from water, a pair builds their nest with grass and down. Like many species of ducks, the drab female alone incubates the 7 to 12 eggs for up to 25 days. Barr Lake State Park and West Quincy Lakes are favorite nesting places where females can be seen carefully leading their fluffy ducklings through bulrushes and across small ponds.

Similar Species: Ruddy Duck (p. 39) has a white cheek and a blue bill. Female Blue-winged Teal (p. 31) is grayer.

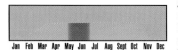

Jan Feb Mar Apr May Jun Jul Aug Sept Oct Nov Dec

Quick I.D.: small duck. *In flight:* blue and green wing patches. *Male:* cinnamon body; red eyes. *Female:* mottled brown overall; broad bill.
Size: 15–16 in.

Northern Shoveler
Anas clypeata

The Northern Shoveler's shovel-like bill stands out among dabbling ducks. The species name *clypeata* is Latin for 'furnished with a shield' and refers to this strikingly distinctive feature. The comb-like structures along the bill's edges and its broad, flat shape allow a shoveler to strain small plants and invertebrates from the water's surface or from muddy substrates. Its diet may not be a culinary marvel, but the abundance of its food source enables the shoveler to commonly breed throughout our area.

Many novice birders become interested in birds because they realize the great variety of ducks in their city parks. Some ducks, like the Northern Shoveler, are dabblers, which prefer shallow water, are not opposed to roaming around on land and lift straight off the water like a helicopter. Many other ducks in the Denver area are divers that are found on large lakes. They can be seen running across the water to gain enough speed for flight. Separating the divers from the dabblers is a first step into the wondrous world of waterfowl.

Similar Species: Mallard (p. 30) and all other dabbling ducks (pp. 29–34) lack the combination of a large bill, a white breast and chestnut sides.

Quick I.D.: mid-sized duck; large bill (longer than head width). *Male:* green head; white breast; chestnut sides. *Female:* mottled brown overall.
Size: 18–20 in.

Jan Feb Mar Apr May Jun Jul Aug Sept Oct Nov Dec

Northern Pintail
Anas acuta

The Northern Pintail is the most elegant duck to be found along shores in the Denver area. The male's long, tapering tail feathers and graceful neck contribute to the sleek appearance of this handsome bird.

Northern Pintails breed commonly in our area. As winter frosts yield to warm spring winds, they are driven through Colorado. By late February, they have arrived in peak numbers, and they are one of the most abundant waterfowl in the state. Until winter again grips our region, pintails are encountered on lakes, fields, ponds and marshes, characteristically 'tipping up' for food and extending their graceful tails skyward. Their hidden nest sites are often great distances from marshes and lakes. After the ducklings hatch, the female might have to march the downy young more than a mile to the sanctuary of a wetland.

Similar Species: Mallard (p. 30), American Wigeon (p. 29) and Gadwall are all chunkier and lack the tapered tail.

Jan Feb Mar Apr May Jun Jul Aug Sept Oct Nov Dec

Quick I.D.: large duck; long, slender neck; long, tapered tail; bluish bill. *In flight:* looks slender and sleek. *Male:* chocolate-brown head; very long tail; white breast and foreneck; dusty gray body. *Female:* mottled light-brown overall.
Size: *Male:* 26–30 in. *Female:* 22–24 in.

Redhead

Aythya americana

Although Redheads are fully equipped with all the features required for diving, they often feed on the surface of wetlands like dabbling ducks. These remarkably handsome ducks can easily be seen casually swimming atop the surface of Standley Lake, Barr Lake and McClellan Reservoir once they have returned from their southern wintering waters.

Although many Redheads in the Denver area are non-breeders, those that do nest occasionally adopt usual nesting strategies: a female Redhead might lay some eggs in another hen's nest and incubate only some of her own. Female Redheads routinely use up more than half of their calcium reserves in egg production.

The Canvasback is another fairly common migrant to our waters. It looks and acts very much like a Redhead, but its back tends to be much whiter and its bill slopes straight up to the forehead. In contrast, the Redhead has a distinct forehead—like it is wearing a ball cap.

Similar Species: Canvasback has a clean white back, and its bill slopes into the forehead. Female Lesser Scaup (p. 36) has more white at the base of the bill.

Quick I.D.: mid-sized duck; rounded head. *Male:* red head; black breast and hind-quarters; gray back and sides; blue-gray bill tipped with black. *Female:* dark overall; light patch bordering black bill tip.
Size: 18–22 in.

Jan Feb Mar Apr May Jun Jul Aug Sept Oct Nov Dec

Lesser Scaup
Aythya affinis

The Lesser Scaup is the Oreo cookie of the duck world—black at both ends and white in the middle. It is a diving duck that prefers deep, open water, and it is common on deep lakes, large rivers and reservoirs. As a result of its diving adaptations, the Lesser Scaup is clumsy on land and during take-off, but it gains dignity when it takes to the water. For close-up views, visit the duck-feeding area along McClellan Reservoir.

Diving ducks have smaller wings, which helps them dive underwater but makes for difficult take-offs and landings. If a duck scoots across the water in an attempt to get airborne, even a first-time birder can tell it's a diver. Divers' legs are placed well back on their bodies—an advantage for underwater swimming—so in order for diving ducks to stand, they must raise their heavy front ends high to maintain balance.

Similar Species: Greater Scaup has a green tinge to its rounded head and a long white stripe on the trailing edge of its wing (seen in flight), and its head is more rounded. Ring-necked Duck has a white shoulder slash and a black back.

Jan Feb Mar Apr May Jun Jul Aug Sept Oct Nov Dec

Quick I.D.: small duck; peaked head. *Male:* dark head with hints of purple; gray back, black breast and hindquarters; dirty white sides; blue-gray bill. *Female:* dark brown; well-defined white patch at base of bill.
Size: 15–17 in.

Common Goldeneye
Bucephala clangula

Although Common Goldeneyes don't breed in the Denver area, they are locally common from late fall right up to their spring migration. Their courtship antics, staged on West Quincy Lakes, McClellan Reservoir and just about every other large waterbody from winter through spring, reinforce a pair's bond prior to their migration to northern woodland lakes.

The courtship display of this widespread duck is one of nature's best slapstick routines. The spry male goldeneye rapidly arches his large green head back until his bill points skyward, producing a seemingly painful *kraaaagh*. Completely unaffected by this chiropractic wonder, he repeatedly performs this ritual to mainly disinterested females. The male continually escalates his spring performance, creating a comedic scene that is most appreciated by birdwatchers.

Similar Species: Bufflehead and Hooded Merganser both lack the round, white face patch.

Quick I.D.: mid-sized duck. *Male:* large, dark green to black head; round, white cheek patch; white body; black back streaked with white. *Female:* chocolate brown hood; sandy-colored body.
Size: 17–19 in.

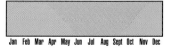

Jan Feb Mar Apr May Jun Jul Aug Sept Oct Nov Dec

Common Merganser
Mergus merganser

Looking like a large jumbo jet taking off, the Common Merganser runs along the surface of the water, beating its heavy wings until sufficient speed is reached for lift-off. Once in the air, our largest duck looks compressed and arrow-like as it flies strongly in low, straight lines.

Mergansers are lean and powerful waterfowl designed for the underwater pursuit of fish. Unlike the bills of other fish-eating birds, a merganser's bill is saw-like, serrated to ensure that its squirmy, slimy prey does not escape.

Common Mergansers are cavity nesters, breeding wherever there are suitable lakes and trees, and they are often seen on rivers. In Denver, Common Mergansers are seen during migration and winter, when these large ducks congregate in rafts in areas of open water such as McClellan Reservoir.

Similar Species: Red-breasted Merganser lacks the white breast and sides. Common Loon (p. 18) has a straight, dark bill and darker sides.

Jan Feb Mar Apr May Jun Jul Aug Sept Oct Nov Dec

Quick I.D.: almost goose-sized. *Male:* well-defined, dark green hood; white body; brilliant orange bill and feet; black spinal streak. *Female:* rusty hood; clean white throat; gray body.
Size: 23–26 in.

Ruddy Duck
Oxyura jamaicensis

♀   ♂

breeding

The clowns of freshwater wetlands, male Ruddy Ducks energetically paddle around their breeding wetlands, displaying with great vigor and beating their breasts with their bright blue beaks. The *plap-plap-plap-plap-plap* sound of their display speeds up until its climax: a spasmodic jerk and sputter. The male's performance occurs from April to the middle of June, and it can readily be seen at Standley Lake.

Many Ruddy Ducks seen in the Denver area remain to breed. The courting pairs find suitable nesting areas and raise anywhere from one to eight young Ruddies. Incredibly, the eggs of these small ducks are almost the same size as those of the much larger Mallard.

By fall, the resident birds, young and returning migrants have lost their distinct color, but they are easily identified by their unique shape and habits. At this time of year, Ruddy Ducks maintain their cocky expression: it seems as though these ducks carry a permanent smile.

Similar Species: All other ducks (pp. 29–38) are generally larger and have shorter tails and relatively smaller heads.

Quick I.D.: small duck; broad bill; large head; tail often cocked up. *Breeding male:* reddish-brown neck and body; black head and tail; white cheek; blue bill. *Non-breeding male:* dull brown overall; dark cap; white cheek. *Female:* like non-breeding male, but each pale cheek has a dark stripe.
Size: 14–16 in.

Jan Feb Mar Apr May Jun Jul Aug Sept Oct Nov Dec

Turkey Vulture
Cathartes aura

Soaring effortlessly above Chatfield State Park, Turkey Vultures ride rising thermals during their afternoon foraging flights. They seldom need to flap their silver-lined wings, and they rock gently from side to side as they carefully scan fields and shorelines for carcasses. Even at great distances, this bare-headed bird can be identified by the way it tends to hold its wings upward in a shallow 'V.'

The Turkey Vulture feeds entirely on carrion, which it can sometimes detect by scent alone. Its head is featherless, which is an adaptation to staying clean and parasite-free while it digs around inside carcasses. This scavenger's well-known habit of regurgitating its rotting meal at intruders may be a defense mechanism: it allows Turkey Vultures to reduce their weight for a quicker take-off, and the smell helps young vultures repel would-be predators.

Similar Species: Hawks (pp. 43–47), eagles (pp. 41 & 42) and Osprey all have large, feathered heads and tend to hold their wings flatter in flight, not in a shallow 'V.'

Quick I.D.: larger than a hawk; sexes similar; all black; small, red head.
In flight: wings held in a shallow 'V'; silver-gray flight feathers; dark wing linings; rocks side to side.
Size: 27–30 in.

Jan Feb Mar Apr May Jun Jul Aug Sept Oct Nov Dec

Bald Eagle
Haliaeetus leucocephalus

The Denver area has been somewhat of a haven for the Bald Eagle in the continental United States. During summer, these birds can be seen easily around Barr Lake; during winter, they tend to collect at Rocky Mountain Arsenal.

Bald Eagles spend most of their time leisurely scanning the landscape from their perch, until they take to the wing to forage. Whether they pluck a duck or fish from the water, pirate prey from another bird or aggressively scavenge at a carcass, actions taken by Bald Eagles are deliberate and decisive.

The decision to select the Bald Eagle as the United States' national symbol was not without controversy. Benjamin Franklin, a very respected naturalist, opposed the decision because of this eagle's habit of scavenging and stealing food from Ospreys. Nevertheless, in many of its habits the Bald Eagle symbolizes nobility, strength and re-sourcefulness. This easily recognized bird is a wondrous source of inspiration to visitors longing for a wilderness connection.

Similar Species: Adult is distinctive. Golden Eagle (p. 42) is similar to immature Bald Eagle, but the Golden Eagle lacks the white mottling in the wings and has a smaller bill, heavily feathered feet (down to the toes) and a golden nape.

Quick I.D.: much larger than a hawk; sexes similar; unfeathered legs.
Adult: white head and tail; dark brown body; yellow beak and feet; yellow eyes.
Immature: brown overall, with some white in body and underwings; dark eyes.
In flight: flaps infrequently; holds wings flat.
Size: 30–43 in.

Jan Feb Mar Apr May Jun Jul Aug Sept Oct Nov Dec

Golden Eagle
Aquila chrysaetos

The regal Golden Eagle, with its sun-bleached, golden nape, is perfectly suited to the landscape in the Denver area. Preferring wild, scenic areas, this 'king of birds' is equally at home coursing low over grasslands or feeling that Rocky Mountain high. Golden Eagles frequently choose nesting sites on cliffs.

The Golden Eagle is more of a predator than its distantly related peer, the Bald Eagle. Golden Eagles are very opportunistic hunters. Their power enables them to prey on animals the size of cranes and pelicans, but rabbits seem to be their preferred food. In recognition of the bird's perceived courage and strength, Native Americans admired and proudly wore Golden Eagle feathers in their headdresses and glorified these hunters in legend.

Similar Species: Immature Bald Eagle (p. 41) lacks the feathers down the legs, shows mottled white in the wings and has a larger head and a heavier bill. Dark phase Red-tailed Hawk (p. 45) is much smaller and has hints of red in the tail.

Quick I.D.: much larger than a hawk; sexes similar; golden tint to the neck and head; fully feathered legs; yellow feet; dark bill; brown eyes. *In flight:* smallish head; long tail; occasional light patches. *Adult:* brown tail is slightly banded with white. *Immature:* white tail base; white patches in wings.
Size: 30–40 in.

Jan Feb Mar Apr May Jun Jul Aug Sept Oct Nov Dec

Northern Harrier

Circus cyaneus

This common marsh hawk can best be identified by its flight behavior: the Northern Harrier traces wavy lines over lush meadows, often retracing its path several times in the quest for prey. Watch the slow, lazy wing beats of the Northern Harrier coincide with its undulating, erratic flight pattern as this raptor skims the willows and bulrushes with its belly. Unlike other hawks, which can find their prey only visually, the Northern Harrier stays close enough to the ground to listen for birds, voles and mice. When movement catches the Harrier's eyes or ears, it abandons its lazy ways to strike at prey with channeled energy.

The harrier's purposeful, low, coursing flights can be observed at Rocky Mountain Arsenal throughout the year. The outstanding courtship flights undertaken as the snows recede are among the most spectacular in the raptorial world. Males fly to considerable heights and perform a series of quick parabolic dives to gain a mate's favor.

Similar Species: Sharp-shinned Hawk (p. 44), Cooper's Hawk, Red-tailed Hawk (p. 45) and Short-eared Owl all lack the white rump.

Quick I.D.: mid-sized hawk; white rump; long tail; long wings; owl-like face (seen only at close range). *Male:* grayish upperparts; whitish underparts; black wing tips. *Female* and *Immature:* brown overall.
Size: 18–22 in.

Jan Feb Mar Apr May Jun Jul Aug Sept Oct Nov Dec

VULTURES, HAWKS & FALCONS 43

Sharp-shinned Hawk
Accipiter striatus

If songbirds dream, the Sharp-shinned Hawk is sure to be the source of their nightmares. These raptors pursue small birds through forests, maneuvering around leaves and branches in the hope of acquiring prey. Sharp-shinned Hawks prey on many birds, with small songbirds and the occasional woodpecker being the most numerous prey items.

These small hawks are easy to find at Cherry Creek and Chatfield state parks when they pass through our area during their fall migration. During the rest of the year, a few of Denver's wooded neighborhoods have a resident 'Sharpie' eager to catch unwary finches, sparrows and starlings. Backyard feeders tend to concentrate sparrows and finches, so they are attractive foraging areas for this small hawk. A sudden eruption of songbirds off the feeder and a few feathers floating on the wind are often the signs of a sudden, successful Sharp-shinned attack.

Similar Species: Cooper's Hawk is usually larger and has a larger head, and its tail is rounded and has a wide terminal band. Merlin has pointed wings and rapid wing beats and lacks the red chest bars.

Jan Feb Mar Apr May Jun Jul Aug Sept Oct Nov Dec

Quick I.D.: pigeon-sized; sexes similar; short, round wings; long tail. *In flight:* flap-and-glide flyer; barred tail is straight at the end with a central notch. *Adult:* blue-gray back; red horizontal streaking on underparts; red eyes. *Immature:* brown overall; vertical, brown streaks on chest; yellow eyes.
Size: 12–14 in. (female larger).

Red-tailed Hawk
Buteo jamaicensis

With its fierce facial expression and untidy feathers, the Red-tailed Hawk looks as though it has been suddenly and rudely awakened. Its characteristic scream further suggests that the Red-tailed Hawk is a bird best avoided. You would think other birds would treat this large raptor with more respect, but the Red-tailed Hawk is constantly being harassed by crows, jays and blackbirds.

It isn't until this hawk is two or three years old that its tail becomes brick red. The dark head, the black 'belt' around its mid-section and the dark leading edge to its wings are better field marks, because they're seen in most Red-tails. In the open country surrounding Chatfield State Park, it's hard not to spot a Red-tail perched on a post or soaring lazily overhead at any time of the year.

Similar Species: Ferruginous Hawk (p. 46) is larger and has a pale head and chestnut booties. Rough-legged Hawk (p. 47) has dark elbow patches and a white tail base. Northern Harrier (p. 43) is slimmer and has a white rump.

Quick I.D.: large hawk; sexes similar; brick-red tail (adult only); brown head; variable brown speckled 'belt'; light flight feathers; dark wing lining and leading edge.
Size: 20–24 in.

Jan Feb Mar Apr May Jun Jul Aug Sept Oct Nov Dec

Ferruginous Hawk
Buteo regalis

Cruising low over the contours of rolling, bare hills around Standley Lake, Ferruginous Hawks seek out ground squirrel or prairie dog communities. These large, graceful, open-country hawks strike unexpectedly, dropping from the air upon the ever-vigilant rodents.

Ferruginous Hawks were once shot and poisoned because they were thought to be pests that preyed on valuable stock. Because of its largely rabbit and rodent diet, however, the Ferruginous Hawk is actually very beneficial to agriculture. Although they are not as numerous as other local hawks, Denver is one of the very few urban areas that boasts a permanent population of these magnificent raptors. A very large, noble bird, the Ferruginous Hawk is well deserving of the scientific name *regalis*.

Similar Species: Red-tailed Hawk (p. 45) is smaller, has darker underparts and often has a red tail. Rough-legged Hawk (p. 47) is present only in winter and has dark 'elbow' patches. Swainson's Hawk is much smaller and has dark flight feathers and light wing linings.

Quick I.D.: large hawk; sexes similar. *In flight:* dark reddish-brown legs stand out against white belly; mostly white underparts. *Light phase adult:* rusty red upperparts; very light underparts; dark leggings; light head; light tail tipped with rust. *Dark phase adult:* dark underparts; white tail; dark wing linings; light flight feathers. *Immature:* may lack dark 'leggings'.
Size: 22–27 in.

Jan Feb Mar Apr May Jun Jul Aug Sept Oct Nov Dec

Rough-legged Hawk
Buteo lagopus

This Arctic-nesting hawk follows fall frosts south to winter in the Denver area. It is a bird that rarely experiences warm weather, and it is well adapted to cold climates: its feet are fully feathered right down to the toes. Rough-legged Hawks can easily be identified by their behavior, even at great distances: while foraging, they are one of the few large hawks to routinely hover over their prey.

Populations of these hawks cycle with the populations of arctic lemmings. When the number of small mammals is high, Rough-legs can produce up to seven young; in years of low mammal numbers, a pair may be fortunate to produce a single chick. For this reason, certain years produce Rough-leg bonanzas in Denver—every power pole seems to have its hawk. In contrast, low years make Denver-area naturalists work the perimeter of Rocky Mountain Arsenal for a fleeting view of this visitor from the tundra.

Similar Species: Red-tailed (p. 45), Ferruginous (p. 46) and Swainson's hawks rarely hover, and adults lack the dark 'elbow' patches and the dark, banded tail. Northern Harrier (p. 43) has a slimmer body, a long tail and a facial disc.

Quick I.D.: large hawk; sexes similar; feet feathered to toes. *In flight:* light underwings with dark 'elbow' patches; long, wings are angled back. *Light phase adult:* light, black-tipped tail; wide, dark 'belt'; streaked breast; dark upperparts; light head. *Dark phase adult:* dark wing linings, body and underparts; light flight feathers and undertail; very dark tail. *Immature:* unstreaked breast; unmarked undertail.
Size: 19–24 in.

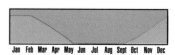

Jan Feb Mar Apr May Jun Jul Aug Sept Oct Nov Dec

American Kestrel
Falco sparverius

This small, noisy falcon is a common sight over much of the Denver area. It has adapted well to rural life, and it is commonly seen perched on power lines, watching for unwary grasshoppers, birds and rodents. When not perched, the American Kestrel can often be seen hovering above potential prey, often orienting itself into the wind. American Kestrels may be encountered in Cherry Creek or Chatfield state parks, and they typically leave their power line perches if vehicles stop nearby.

All falcons are skilled hunters, and they have a unique, tooth-like projection on their hooked bills that can quickly crush the neck of small prey. The American Kestrel's species name *sparverius* is Latin for 'pertaining to sparrows,' an occasional prey item. This trait was also represented in its former name (still occasionally used) 'Sparrow Hawk.'

Similar Species: Sharp-shinned Hawk (p. 44) and Cooper's Hawk have short, rounded wings. Merlin is slightly larger, has a banded tail and has boldly streaked underparts.

Quick I.D.: robin-sized; long, pointed wings; long tail; two vertical, black stripes on each side of face; spotted breast; hooked bill. *In flight:* rapid wing beats. *Male:* blue wings; russet back; colorful head. *Female:* russet back and wings.
Size: 8–9 in.

Jan Feb Mar Apr May Jun Jul Aug Sept Oct Nov Dec

Prairie Falcon
Falco mexicanus

Prairie Falcons blaze across prairie skies, their keen eyes ever vigilant for food items. With four common falcon species, Denver is falcon heaven, and the Prairie is definitely one of the signature birds in our area. These birds are extremely fast, exceptionally maneuverable and can be encountered with a little work every day of the year in our prairie outskirts. The U.S. Air Force Academy has paid homage to this bird's aerial skill by declaring it as their official mascot.

Like Peregrines, Prairie Falcons choose steep cliffs upon which to nest. These protected sites, known as eyries, are used repeatedly, and they are easily spotted along undisturbed river courses, because they are generally stained white. During summer, Prairie Falcons favor a diet of small mammals; during winter, however, their tastes turn to small birds, such as Horned Larks, found in farmlands.

Similar Species: Peregrine Falcon (p. 50) lacks the dark 'wing pits' and has a wide mustache and a dark hood. Merlin is much smaller and lacks the black 'wing pits.'

Quick I.D.: smaller than a crow; sexes similar; brown upperparts; light face with two dark brown, narrow facial stripes; underparts white with brown spotting. *In flight:* black 'wing pits'; pointed wings; long, narrow, banded tail; quick wing beats.
Size: *Male:* 14–15 in. *Female:* 17–18 in.

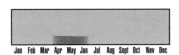

Jan Feb Mar Apr May Jun Jul Aug Sept Oct Nov Dec

VULTURES, HAWKS & FALCONS 49

Peregrine Falcon
Falco peregrinus

The Peregrine Falcon is one of the fastest animals in the world, and it can reach speeds of up to 100 miles an hour. Once a Peregrine has its prey singled out, even the fastest ducks and shorebirds have little chance of outflying this effective predator. The Peregrine Falcon plunges on its prey, punching large birds in mid-air and following them to the ground, where they are killed and eaten.

Denver's Peregrines declined to near extinction because of pesticide residues in the environment. An active recovery plan for this endangered species has restored the population, and this magnificent bird can now be found breeding on downtown skyscrapers. These artificial cliffs seem to duplicate their natural nesting requirements, and the numerous prey species in the area also contribute to their nesting success. It is pleasantly ironic that within some of America's most developed habitats, the noble Peregrine has found sanctuary from possible extinction.

Similar Species: Prairie Falcon (p. 49) has dark 'wing pits' and lacks the dark hood. Merlin and American Kestrel (p. 48) are much smaller.

Quick I.D.: crow-sized; sexes similar. *In flight:* pointed wings; long tail. *Adult:* dark blue hood extending down cheek; steel-blue upperparts; light underparts with dark speckles. *Immature:* like adult, except brown where adult is steel-blue; more heavily streaked underparts.
Size: 15–20 in.

Jan Feb Mar Apr May Jun Jul Aug Sept Oct Nov Dec

Ring-necked Pheasant
Phasianus colchicus

These spectacular birds, which were introduced from Asia, are common in dense, weedy fields in the Denver region. The *pe-cok* calls of male pheasants sound like a squeaky gate. They rise from shrubs at Cherry Creek, often surprising leisurely walkers.

During the breeding season, males collect a harem of up to five hens, which they then attempt to protect from the advances of rival males. Males are armed with a short but dangerous spur on the back of the leg, and fights between them can be fierce. Once males have mated with the harem, the females occasionally deposit their eggs into one communal nest. Whether overflowing with multiple clutches or not, pheasant nests are frequently preyed upon by Denver's native fauna.

Similar Species: Male is distinctive. Female Blue Grouse (p. 52) has a shorter tail.

♂

Quick I.D.: hawk-sized; long, tapering tail; short, round wings. *Male:* iridescent green hood; fleshy red skin on cheek; white 'necklace'; golden-red body plumage. *Female:* brown overall.
Size: *Male:* 31–35 in. *Female:* 21–24 in.

Jan Feb Mar Apr May Jun Jul Aug Sept Oct Nov Dec

Blue Grouse
Dendragapus obscurus

The Blue Grouse performs its annual courtship song in the dense foothill forests of the Rockies. The male's voice is so deep that the human ear can hear only a fraction of the sounds. The low frequency travels well through the conifer forest, however, and the owl-like hooting attracts an audience of female Blue Grouse to the male's simple courtship dance. A female shows her approval with a series of cackling notes. This auditory reinforcement is so stimulating to males that they have been known to intimately investigate tape machines playing a female's response.

Blue Grouse make seasonal migrations, but rather than moving north-south, they simply move up and down mountain slopes. Grouse do not occur in the immediate area of Denver, but they are frequently encountered year-round in the transition zone and subalpine areas just west of the city limits. They tend to be met on trails, where they appear quite tame, cautiously eating a few conifer needles before moving off the trail.

Similar Species: White-tailed Ptarmigan is smaller and has white outer tail feathers.

Quick I.D.: hawk-sized; dark overall. *Male:* orange comb over each eye; purple throat patches surrounded by white feathers (during courtship). *Female:* mottled brown and gray.
Size: *Male:* 17–19 in. *Female:* 18–22 in.

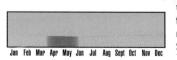

Jan Feb Mar Apr May Jun Jul Aug Sept Oct Nov Dec

Wild Turkey
Meleagris gallopavo

♂

Wild Turkeys are wary birds with refined senses and a highly developed social system, so predators can seldom sneak up on a flock. Although turkeys prefer to stay on the ground—they are able to run 20 miles an hour—they can fly short distances, and they often roost in trees for the night. These successful social birds produce a wide array of sounds, but only a courting male gives the classic loud *gobble*.

Male Turkeys (gobblers) grow breast sponges just prior to the breeding season. This mass of fibrous tissue, weighing up to two pounds, serves as an energy reservoir for the bird, which might eat very little during the courtship season.

The Wild Turkey was Benjamin Franklin's choice for America's national emblem. It lost to the Bald Eagle by one ballot in a congressional vote. The Wild Turkey is one of the few domesticated agricultural animals that originated in the New World.

Similar Species: None.

Quick I.D.: larger than a goose; naked red-blue head; dark, glossy, iridescent body plumage; copper tail tipped in dirty white; unfeathered legs. *Male:* long central breast feather; more colorful on head and body; red wattles. *Female:* blue-gray head; less iridescent body.
Size: *Male:* 48–50 in. *Female:* 35–37 in.

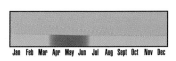

Jan Feb Mar Apr May Jun Jul Aug Sept Oct Nov Dec

Killdeer

Charadrius vociferus

The Killdeer is probably the most widespread shorebird in the Denver area. It nests on gravelly shorelines, utility rights-of-way, lawns, pastures and occasionally on gravel roofs and parking lots in cities. Its name is a paraphrase of its distinctive, loud call: *kill-dee kill-dee kill-deer.*

The Killdeer's response to predators relies on deception and good acting skills. To divert a predator's attention away from a nest or a brood of young, an adult Killdeer (like many shorebirds) will flop around to fake an injury (usually a broken wing or leg). Once the Killdeer has the attention of the fox, crow, gull or human, it leads the predator away from the vulnerable nest. After it reaches a safe distance, the adult Killdeer is suddenly 'healed' and flies off, leaving the predator confused and without a meal.

Similar Species: Semipalmated Plover has only one breast band, is smaller and is found mostly on mudflats.

Jan Feb Mar Apr May Jun Jul Aug Sept Oct Nov Dec

Quick I.D.: robin-sized; sexes similar; two black bands across breast; brown back; russet rump; long legs; white underparts. **Size:** 9–11 in.

American Avocet
Recurvirostra americana

An American Avocet in full breeding plumage may be the most elegant bird in North America. To some birders, its graceful features and striking colors are unmatched. During courtship, the female avocet extends her dainty bill forward and lowers her chin until it just clears the water's surface. The male struts around his statuesque mate until conditions are perfect; then the male jumps atop the motionless female and the pair quickly mates. After the male dismounts, the pair cross their slender bills and walk together in unison, reinforcing their bond.

Foraging American Avocets sweep their partially open bills from side to side, whipping them through the water's surface. They are capable of picking up minute crustaceans, aquatic insects and the occasional seed with this odd foraging technique.

Similar Species: Black-necked Stilt has a straight black bill, red legs and a black neck and head.

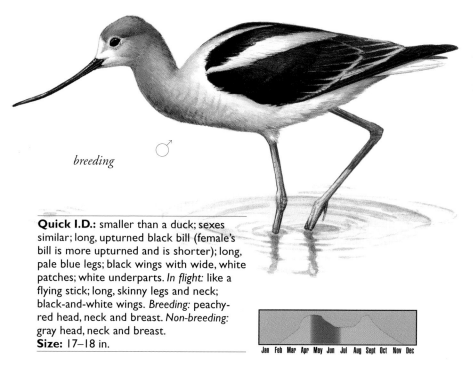

breeding

♂

Quick I.D.: smaller than a duck; sexes similar; long, upturned black bill (female's bill is more upturned and is shorter); long, pale blue legs; black wings with wide, white patches; white underparts. *In flight:* like a flying stick; long, skinny legs and neck; black-and-white wings. *Breeding:* peachy-red head, neck and breast. *Non-breeding:* gray head, neck and breast.
Size: 17–18 in.

Jan Feb Mar Apr May Jun Jul Aug Sept Oct Nov Dec

Lesser Yellowlegs
Tringa flavipes

On a spring walk along the shores of Barr Lake, you will encounter several sandpipers. The Lesser Yellowlegs prefers shallow pools where it can peck for small invertebrates, but it may venture belly-deep into the water to pursue prey. Occasionally, a yellowlegs can be seen hopping along on one leg, with the other one tucked up in the body feathers to reduce heat loss.

Many birders enjoy the challenge of distinguishing the Lesser Yellowlegs from the Greater Yellowlegs. The Greater, which is less common in our area (but don't let that bias your identification), has a relatively longer, heavier bill. Its bill is also slightly upturned—so slightly that you notice it one moment and not the next. Generally, the Lesser calls with two *tews*, and the Greater calls with three. Many experienced birders will name them at a glance, but others are satisfied in writing 'unidentified yellowlegs' in their field notes.

Similar Species: Greater Yellowlegs is larger and has a longer, upturned bill.

breeding

Jan Feb Mar Apr May Jun Jul Aug Sept Oct Nov Dec

Quick I.D.: robin-sized; sexes similar; long, bright yellow legs; finely streaked, gray body; bill is shorter than head width.
Size: 9–11 in.

Spotted Sandpiper

Actitis macularia

breeding

This common shorebird of lakes and rivers has a most uncommon mating strategy. In a reversal of the gender roles of most birds, female Spotted Sandpipers compete for males. After the nest is built and the eggs are laid, the female leaves to find another mate, while the first male is left to incubate the eggs. This behavior can be repeated two or more times before the female settles down with one male to raise her last brood of chicks.

Spotted Sandpipers nest in the Denver area, and they are frequently encountered during the migratory months along the undisturbed shores of Barr Lake and McClellan Reservoir.

Spotted Sandpipers are readily identified by their arthritic-looking, stiff-winged flight low over water. Their peppy calls—*eat-wheat wheat-wheat-wheat*—burst from startled birds as they retreat over the water from shoreline disturbances. Spotted Sandpipers constantly teeter and bob when not in flight.

Similar Species: Killdeer (p. 54) has dark throat bands. Solitary Sandpiper has an eye ring and lacks the prominent breast spots. Lesser Yellowlegs (p. 56) has longer legs.

Quick I.D.: smaller than a robin; sexes similar; often teeters and bobs; yellow legs. *Breeding:* spotted breast (more pronounced in female); olive-gray back; yellow bill tipped with black. *Non-breeding:* plain white underparts.
Size: 7–8 in.

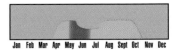

Jan Feb Mar Apr May Jun Jul Aug Sept Oct Nov Dec

Baird's Sandpiper
Calidris bairdii

The Baird's Sandpiper is a modest-looking shorebird with extraordinary migratory habits. It flies all the way from South America to the Arctic and back every year, stopping off at mudflats along the way to fuel its flight muscles. It is but one of many shorebirds that share this migratory lifestyle, and because of their movements they are known collectively as 'wind birds.'

When the wind birds descend from the skies upon the shorelines of Barr Lake, the challenge of identifying migrating shorebirds awaits the interested birder. In May and then again in August through September, many species of these confusing 'peeps' (as they are also known by birders) can be observed with patience and at quite close range. Even if the subtlety of plumage is not your primary interest, a morning spent with shuffling sandpipers will prove enjoyable.

Similar Species: Pectoral Sandpiper has sharply delineated chest markings. Least Sandpiper has light-colored legs and is smaller.

breeding

Quick I.D.: smaller than a robin; sexes similar; black legs and bill; wings extend beyond tail; faint, buff-brown breast speckling; large black patterns on back and wing covers.
Size: 7–7^1/$_2$ in.

Jan Feb Mar Apr May Jun Jul Aug Sept Oct Nov Dec

Long-billed Dowitcher
Limnodromus scolopaceus

When cool fall air descends from the north, shorebirds concentrate in large numbers along the shores of Barr Lake. The oncoming winter forces dowitchers and other shorebirds to retreat to the south, often packing them together in large numbers along the way. Dowitchers tend to be stockier than most of their neighboring shorebirds, and they avoid deeper water. The sewing machine–like rhythms that dowitchers perform while foraging deeply into the mudflats is helpful for field identification.

Long-billed Dowitchers have shorter wings than most of the other long-distance migrant shorebirds in our area, but they don't seem to suffer any loss in flight speed. Dowitchers pack closely together to feed in knee-deep water, and it is thought that their short wings make it more practical for the birds to take flight from these crowded pools. From their rhythmic flights to their stitching foraging probes, Long-billed Dowitchers are among the most engaging shorebirds to pass through our area.

Similar Species: Common Snipe (p. 60) has longer legs, heavily barred upperparts and different foraging techniques.

non-breeding

Quick I.D.: robin-sized; sexes similar; very long, straight, dark bill; very stocky body; short neck. *Breeding:* reddish underparts; lightly barred flanks; dark, mottled upperparts; dark eye line; light eyebrow; dark yellow legs; white rump. *Non-breeding:* gray overall; white belly.
Size: 11–12¹/₂ in. (female larger).

Jan Feb Mar Apr May Jun Jul Aug Sept Oct Nov Dec

Common Snipe
Gallinago gallinago

Common Snipes have startled many walkers as they stroll along Cherry Creek and other Denver-area wetlands. These shorebirds are both secretive and well camouflaged, so few people notice them until the birds fly suddenly out of nearby grassy tussocks. As soon as snipes take to the air, they perform a series of quick zigzags, an evasive maneuver designed to confuse predators. Snipes are seldom seen in large groups, nor are they normally encountered along open shorelines; their heavily streaked plumage is suited to grassy habitats.

The mystical 'winnowing' sound of courting Common Snipes is heard infrequently in the Denver area, because their breeding habitat has largely been destroyed. During spring evenings at Barr Lake, however, the accelerating sound, produced in flight by air passing through spread tail feathers, can thrill perceptive observers.

Similar Species: All other shorebirds are either too short of bill or not as heavily streaked.

Jan Feb Mar Apr May Jun Jul Aug Sept Oct Nov Dec

Quick I.D.: robin-sized; sexes similar; long, black-tipped bill; heavily streaked back; short neck; striped head; long legs.
Size: $10^1/_2$–$11^1/_2$ in.

Wilson's Phalarope
Phalaropus tricolor

Not only are phalaropes the most colorful of the shorebirds; they are also the most unusual. These intriguing birds practice a mating strategy known as polyandry—each female mates with several males—which is extremely rare throughout the animal kingdom. The brightly colored female phalarope defends the nest site from other females and leaves her mates to tend the eggs. This breeding strategy is unusual because it takes a massive amount of energy for a female to produce eggs, and normally it would be to the female's advantage to see the process to completion. In one of nature's greatest role reversals, however, female phalaropes entrust the males with rearing the young. Even Audubon was fooled by the phalarope's breeding habits; he mislabeled the female and male birds in all of his illustrations.

When foraging, phalaropes are very easily identified, because they tend to get in over their heads and spin madly. In deep water phalaropes twirl in tight circles, pecking at the water's surface for organisms churned up by the shorebird's vortex.

Similar Species: Red-necked Phalarope has a dark head and back and is a migrant through the Rockies. Lesser Yellowlegs (p. 56) has yellow legs and streaked underparts.

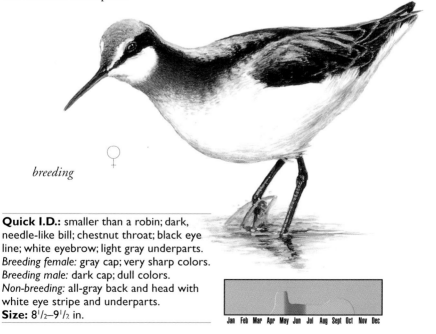

breeding

Quick I.D.: smaller than a robin; dark, needle-like bill; chestnut throat; black eye line; white eyebrow; light gray underparts.
Breeding female: gray cap; very sharp colors.
Breeding male: dark cap; dull colors.
Non-breeding: all-gray back and head with white eye stripe and underparts.
Size: 8¹/₂–9¹/₂ in.

Jan Feb Mar Apr May Jun Jul Aug Sept Oct Nov Dec

Franklin's Gull
Larus pipixcan

Franklin's Gulls refuse to be seduced by the seas and oceans of the world. Rather, these gulls favor the open prairies, following tractors and ploughs in the same manner as their cousins follow schooners and factory ships. They still return to wetlands to nest, but in their foraging wanderings they feed on the multitude of insects and other invertebrates inhabiting our grasslands.

Franklin's Gulls are also affectionately known as 'Prairie Doves.' This name is appealing because these gulls share with doves soft voices and rounded physiques. Their neat, black hoods highlight their inquisitive eye rings, giving them a look of innocence. In addition, males in their spring dress are occasionally awash with faint pink highlights upon the breast.

Franklin's Gulls tend to avoid the hectic pace of urban life, but they can frequently be encountered during summer or migrating overhead at Barr Lake or other area wetlands.

Similar Species: Adult Bonaparte's Gull has a black bill and shows more white in its wings.

breeding

Quick I.D.: small gull; sexes similar; gray mantle; white eye ring; black wing tips with white spots; white underparts.
Breeding: black head; red bill; breast often has a pinkish tinge; red-orange legs.
Non-breeding: white head; dark patch on the back of the head; black legs
Size: 13–15 in.

Jan Feb Mar Apr May Jun Jul Aug Sept Oct Nov Dec

Ring-billed Gull
Larus delawarensis

This widespread gull, which is extremely common in the Denver area, carries a distinctive dark bill ring, for which it is well named. The Ring-billed Gull is a common sight in cities: it is frequently seen in parks or effortlessly soaring high overhead. The warm air rising from concrete and asphalt is like an elevator that dozens of gulls ride simultaneously, climbing until their sleek shapes vanish into the sky.

Although these gulls appear to be regular urbanites, like so many people in Denver, they commute daily into the cities. From shoreline suburbs, gull traffic can be seen during the early morning, congested along the skyways leading into town. Their daily activities involve squabbling with other greedy gulls over leftovers from fast-food restaurants and for food in open areas. When nicely fed, they may break from feeding duties by soaring high above the hectic pace of city life.

Similar Species: California Gull (p. 64) lacks the bill ring and has dark eyes and greenish legs. Herring Gull is larger, has pink legs and lacks the bill ring. Franklin's Gull (p. 62) is smaller and has a black hood in breeding plumage and a black ear patch in non-breeding plumage.

breeding

Quick I.D.: mid-sized gull; sexes similar; black ring near bill tip; yellow bill and legs; dark gray wings; light eyes; black wing tips; small white spots on black primaries; white underparts. *Non-breeding:* white head and nape washed with brown. *First winter:* mottled grayish brown; gray back; blackish-brown primaries; brown band on tail.
Size: 18–20 in.

Jan Feb Mar Apr May Jun Jul Aug Sept Oct Nov Dec

California Gull
Larus californicus

California Gulls are generally spotted by accident. Even most serious birders tend to disregard gulls as everyday birds, but every now and then, a wandering eye will spot a bird that lacks the tell-tale black bill ring and looks back with a dark eye. 'Oh! a California Gull,' some will say. But after a few seconds of pondering the birds, most people move on without acknowledging this bird's monumental contributions to the West.

In 1848 and 1855, Utah's harvests were threatened by swarms of grass-hoppers until large numbers of California Gulls mercifully appeared, ate the pests and saved the crops. The birds enabled the pioneers to harvest a crop, and, in recognition, a monument in Salt Lake City and the state bird title honor this prairie gull.

In our area, California Gulls tend to nest communally on low-lying islands and isolated beaches. Their simple scrapes are generally placed no closer than the distance two gulls can bridge with aggressive bill jabs from atop their nests. From these breeding colonies, adults forage great distances, entering Denver and combing farmlands for food for their young.

Similar Species: Adult Ring-billed Gull (p. 63) has light eyes and a black ring around its bill. Adult Herring Gull is much larger and has light eyes and pink legs.

breeding

Jan Feb Mar Apr May Jun Jul Aug Sept Oct Nov Dec

Quick I.D.: mid-sized gull; sexes similar. *Adult:* white head; yellow bill and legs; dark eyes; red and black spots on the lower mandible tip; dark gray back; black wing tips; black primaries with small white spots; white underparts. *Immature:* mottled brown.

Size: 18–20 in.

Black Tern
Chlidonias niger

Over cattail marshes, the erratic, aeronautic flight of the Black Tern is unmatched by any other bird. Black Terns dip, dive, swoop and spin in dizzying foraging flights, picking insects neatly off the water's surface. These terns are masters of the airways above their marshy breeding grounds. They take only brief breaks to perch on a nearby post or to return to their nests.

Black Terns build their nests deep in the cattails and bulrushes at Barr Lake and other area marshes. The nest is set atop a muskrat lodge or another floating platform. Both parents incubate the clutch of two to four eggs and then help feed the quickly growing young.

Black Terns look like frail birds, but they are built to have dominion over the winds. When they leave our area in September, they head out to tropical coasts, to dance over foreign waters until their spring return.

Similar Species: Common Tern and Forster's Tern are much lighter underneath. Barn Swallow (p. 84) is much smaller and has a shorter bill and lighter underparts.

breeding

Quick I.D.: robin-sized; sexes similar; gray upperparts; gray tail; black bill; long, pointed wings; shallowly forked tail; reddish-black legs. *Breeding:* black head, neck and underparts; white undertail coverts. *Non-breeding:* white underparts; black mark behind eye; dark gray collar on sides in front of wings.
Size: 9–11 in.

Jan Feb Mar Apr May Jun Jul Aug Sept Oct Nov Dec

Rock Dove
Columba livia

The Rock Dove (or 'Pigeon') is the ruling king (or queen) of the urban canyon. It has taken to nesting and roosting on our skyscrapers, bridges and other buildings more readily than any other bird species. This Eurasian native, first brought to North America in 1606 as a food source, has turned the tables on humans: it routinely feasts on our handouts and leftovers.

Rock Doves may appear strained when walking—their heads move back and forth with every step—but few birds are as agile in flight, or as abundant in urban and industrial areas. While no other bird varies as much in coloration, all Rock Doves, whether white, red, blue or mixed-pigment, will clap their wings above and below their bodies upon take-off.

Similar Species: Mourning Dove (p. 67) is the same length, but it is slender and has a long, tapering tail and olive-brown plumage.

Jan Feb Mar Apr May Jun Jul Aug Sept Oct Nov Dec

Quick I.D.: mid-sized pigeon; sexes similar; variable color (iridescent blue-gray, black, red or white); white rump (usually); orange feet; fleshy base to bill.
Size: 13–14 in.

Mourning Dove
Zenaida macroura

As a Mourning Dove bursts into flight, its wings 'clap' above and below its body for the first few wing beats. The Mourning Dove is a swift, direct flyer, and its wings can be heard whistling through the air. When this bird is not in flight, its peaceful *cooah-coo-coo-coo* call can be heard filtering through open woodlands. These year-round residents roost inconspicuously in trees, but their soft cooing often betrays their presence.

The Mourning Dove feeds primarily on the ground, picking up grain and grit in open areas and visiting many backyard feeders. It builds a flat, loose stick nest that rests flimsily on branches and trunks. Mourning Doves are attentive parents and, like other members of the pigeon family, they feed 'milk' to their young. It isn't true milk—birds lack mammary glands—but a fluid produced by glands in the bird's crop. The chicks insert their bills down the adult's throat to drink the thick liquid.

Similar Species: Rock Dove (p. 66) has a white rump, is stockier and has a shorter, broader tail.

Quick I.D.: jay-sized; sexes similar; gray-brown plumage; long, white-trimmed, tapering tail; sleek body; dark, shiny patch below ear; orange feet; dark bill; buff-colored underparts.
Size: 11–13 in.

Jan Feb Mar Apr May Jun Jul Aug Sept Oct Nov Dec

Flammulated Owl

Otus flammeolus

The Flammulated Owl is probably quite common, but this small owl is so effective at eluding birdwatchers that any encounter is prized. During the day, this tiny owl presses itself up against pine trees, its mottled pattern blending perfectly with the bark's texture. It is only during spring nights—when the birds offer soft, deep and persistent hoots from their mountainous lofts—that an encounter is likely.

The Flammulated Owl appears to favor an insectivorous diet more than most other woodland owls in our area. Although this may not seem odd, its style of swooping and seizing insects in mid-air is certainly unconventional. As a result of this preference for insects, they are forced out of our region during the coldest parts of our year, migrating south into Mexico.

Similar Species: Eastern Screech-Owl has light-colored eyes and larger ear tufts.

gray phase

Jan Feb Mar Apr May Jun Jul Aug Sept Oct Nov Dec

Quick I.D.: small owl; sexes similar; small ear tufts; dark eyes; rufous facial disk; dark bill; vertical breast streaks; gray-brown overall; white eyebrow.
Size: 6–7 in.

Great Horned Owl
Bubo virginianus

The Great Horned Owl, the most widely distributed owl in North America, is among the most formidable of predators. It uses specialized hearing, powerful talons and human-sized eyes during nocturnal hunts for mice, rabbits, quails, amphibians and occasionally fish. It has a poorly developed sense of smell, which is why it can prey on skunks. Worn-out and discarded Great Horned Owl feathers are therefore often identifiable by a simple sniff.

The deep, resonant hooting of the Great Horned Owl is easily imitated, often leading to interesting exchanges between bird and birder. The call's deep tone is not as distinctive as its pace, however, which closely follows the rhythm of *Eat my food, I'll-eat yooou.*

Similar Species: Eastern Screech-Owl is much smaller and has vertical breast streaking. Long-eared Owl has a slimmer body and vertical streaks on its chest, and its ear tufts are very close together.

Quick I.D.: hawk-sized; sexes similar; large, widely spaced ear tufts; fine, horizontal chest bars; dark brown plumage; white throat.
Size: 18–25 in.

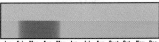

Jan Feb Mar Apr May Jun Jul Aug Sept Oct Nov Dec

Burrowing Owl
Athene cunicularia

If you gaze out over the prairie dog town at Cherry Creek, Rocky Mountain Arsenal or a handful of other locales in our area, an ill-behaved 'dog' might catch your eye. Not a prairie dog at all, the Burrowing Owl is a neighbor to these social rodents, living alongside them in subterranean burrows. At a distance, Burrowing Owls can look very similar to prairie dogs, but carefull inspection will reveal these owls' yellow eyes, long legs and perky disposition.

Burrowing Owl populations are declining in our area. The conversion of native grasslands to cropland has reduced the breeding range of these birds, and certain chemicals used in agriculture have been known to decrease breeding success. Their close association with prairie dogs has not benefited them either, because they have often been killed as victims of mistaken identity.

Burrowing Owls are among the prairie's purest inhabitants, scorning treed habitat in favor of wide open spaces. During their brief stay they feed their large, rapidly growing families on insects, small rodents and occasionally birds.

Similar Species: Short-eared Owl has a heavily streaked breast, short legs and long wings, and it doesn't nest in burrows.

Quick I.D.: smaller than a robin; sexes similar; long legs; rounded head; no ear tufts; yellow bill; short wings. *Adult:* white spotting on breast; brown upperparts flecked with white. *Immature:* buff-brown breast is unspotted.
Size: 8–9 in.

Jan Feb Mar Apr May Jun Jul Aug Sept Oct Nov Dec

Common Nighthawk
Cordeiles minor

The Common Nighthawk, which is unrelated to true hawks, has a Dr. Jekyll and Mr. Hyde persona: mild-mannered by day, it rests on the ground or on a horizontal tree branch, its color and shape blending perfectly into the texture of the bark. At dusk, the Common Nighthawk takes on a new form as a dazzling and erratic flyer, catching insects in flight.

To many people, the sounds of the nighthawk are the sound of summer evenings, and the recent declines in their numbers have left many naturalists longing for the previously common calls. The fascinating courtship of Common Nighthawks occurs over forest openings, grass-lands and urban areas. The nighthawks repeatedly call out with a loud, nasal *peeent* as they circle high overhead, then they dive suddenly toward the ground and create a hollow 'vroom' sound by thrusting their wings forward at the last possible moment, pulling out of the dive.

Similar Species: Common Poorwill has rounded wings and tail.

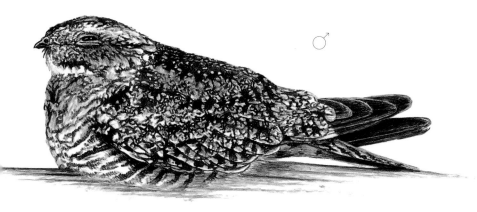

Quick I.D.: robin-sized; cryptic, light to dark brown plumage; white wrist bands.
In flight: shallowly forked tail; long, pointed wings; flight is erratic. *Male:* white throat; white tail band. *Female:* buffy throat; no tail band.
Size: 9–10 in.

Jan Feb Mar Apr May Jun Jul Aug Sept Oct Nov Dec

Belted Kingfisher
Ceryle alcyon

The Belted Kingfisher is found year-round near quiet waters, never far from shore. As their name suggests, kingfishers primarily prey on fish, which they catch with precise, headfirst dives. A dead branch extending over water will often serve as a perch from which they can survey the fish below.

The Belted Kingfisher builds its nest near the end of a long tunnel excavated a few feet into sandy or dirt banks. Its rattling call (similar to a teacup shaking on a saucer), blue-gray coloration and large crest are the distinctive features of the Belted Kingfisher. With most bird species, the males are more colorful, but female kingfishers are distinguished from males by the presence of a second, rust-colored band across the belly.

Although there are many species of kingfisher in the world, the Belted Kingfisher is the only member of its family found across most of the United States. Where open water is found in the Denver area, Belted Kingfishers can be encountered any day of the year, crashing into calm waters in search of fish.

Similar Species: None.

Quick I.D.: pigeon-sized; blue-gray back, wings and head; shaggy crest; heavy bill. *Male:* single, blue chest band. *Female:* blue chest band and rust-colored 'belt.'
Size: 12–14 in.

Jan Feb Mar Apr May Jun Jul Aug Sept Oct Nov Dec

Downy Woodpecker
Picoides pubescens

Soft taps carry through a quiet forest, sounding out the activities of a Downy Woodpecker. It searches for hidden invertebrates methodically, chipping off dead bark and probing into crevices. The woodpecker's small bill is amazingly effective at removing tiny slabs of bark, which rain down to the forest floor. The Downy Woodpecker is a systematic forager, and because of its small bill, it can find food that larger-billed woodpeckers cannot reach. Only when all the nooks of a tree have been probed will the Downy look about and give a chipper note before moving on to explore neighboring trees.

This black-and-white bird is the smallest North American woodpecker, and it is common along the Highline Canal. It's easily attracted to backyard feeders by suet. The male is readily distinguished from the female by a small patch of red feathers on the back of his head.

Similar Species: Hairy Woodpecker is larger and has a longer bill and clean white outer tail feathers.

Quick I.D.: large sparrow–sized; black-and-white wings and back; unmarked, white underparts; short, stubby bill; white outer tail feathers are spotted black. *Male:* red patch on back of head. *Female:* no red patch.
Size: 6–7 in.

Jan Feb Mar Apr May Jun Jul Aug Sept Oct Nov Dec

Northern Flicker
Colaptes auratus

Walkers strolling along the Highland Canal may be surprised by a woodpecker flushing from the ground before them. As the Northern Flicker beats a hasty retreat, it reveals an unmistakable white rump and red wing linings. It is the least arboreal of our woodpeckers, and it spends more time feeding on the ground than in trees. Often, it is only when the Northern Flicker is around its nest cavity in a tree that it truly behaves like other woodpeckers: clinging, rattling and drumming.

The Northern Flicker can easily be seen all year, and it occasionally visits backyard feeders. Northern Flickers (and other birds) squash ants and then preen themselves with the remains. (Ants contain concentrations of formic acid, which is believed to kill small parasites living on the flicker's skin and in its feathers.)

Similar Species: Other woodpeckers (p. 73) and American Robin (p. 101) lack the white rump and the red wing linings.

Jan Feb Mar Apr May Jun Jul Aug Sept Oct Nov Dec

Quick I.D.: jay-sized; brown-barred back; red wing and tail linings; spotted underparts; black bib; white rump; long bill; gray crown; red nape. *Male:* red mustache. *Female:* no mustache.
Size: 11–14 in.

Broad-tailed Hummingbird

Selasphorus platycercus

During the last week of May, the Denver area is the site of a most unusual daily migration. Male Broad-tailed Hummingbirds make daily reconnaissance flights between their alpine breeding grounds and the lower foothills. Although the males stake out and defend their territories in alpine areas, the lack of flowering plants there forces them to feed at lower elevations, where they find flowers, gardens and feeders. Males use their long, tapered primary feathers to produce an eerie, buzzing, cricket-like trill during their courtship flights.

These miniature birds span the ecological gap between birds and insects, feeding on the energy-rich nectar that flower blooms provide in exchange for the feeders' pollinating assistance. Perhaps it is the birds' remarkable size, or their intimate association with flowers, which leads to the inescapable joy carried by these birds upon their tiny wings.

Similar Species: Male Rufous Hummingbird is rusty-red overall. Calliope Hummingbird has a shorter bill and a streaked throat.

Quick I.D.: much smaller than a sparrow; iridescent green upperparts; long, narrow bill; broad tail. *Male:* red throat; white underparts; green flanks. *Female:* pale underparts; peach-colored flanks; white throat.
Size: 4 in.

Jan Feb Mar Apr May Jun Jul Aug Sept Oct Nov Dec

Western Wood-Pewee
Contopus sordidulus

Following this bird's down-slurred call normally leads to the mid-level of the forest. The Western Wood-Pewee calls persistently throughout the day with its plaintive, whistled *peee you*. It chooses a perch beneath the crown of a tree or on a snag, fallen log or branch from which to launch itself in long, looping foraging ventures.

The nest of the Western Wood-Pewee is well camouflaged by both its shape and color: the completed structure resembles a bump on a horizontal limb. Despite this concealing masterpiece, these small flycatchers vigorously defend their nest by chasing and vocally harassing hawks, jays and chipmunks.

Similar Species: Olive-sided Flycatcher has white rump patches and is larger. Willow Flycatcher (p. 77) has a more colorful lower mandible, browner upperparts and lighter underparts.

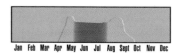

Jan Feb Mar Apr May Jun Jul Aug Sept Oct Nov Dec

Quick I.D.: sparrow-sized; sexes similar; dark olive-brown upperparts; light underparts; two faint, white wing bars; no eye ring; light-colored lower mandible; light undertail coverts; light-colored throat.
Size: 5–6 in.

Willow Flycatcher
Empidonax traillii

Southern spring winds carry the first Willow Flycatchers into Colorado forests in early May. The day of their arrival is often easily recognized because these small birds punctuate their presence with their simple and sneezy *fitz-bew* song. From swaying willow perches, Willow Flycatchers sing and survey their chosen territories.

When threatened, the Willow Flycatcher is one of the boldest and most pugnacious songbirds in the deciduous forests of Colorado. During the nesting season, it is noisy and aggressive, driving away all avian intruders and fighting furiously with rival males.

The confusing collection of *Empidonax* flycatchers are the 'lords of the mosquitoes,' but the curse of the birdwatcher. The Willow, Hammond's and Cordilleran flycatchers all pass through our area, and they are virtually indistinguishable in the field. Their confusing plumage should not deter novice birders, however, because the pleasantness of these small birds overshadows such small details.

Similar Species: Western Wood-Pewee (p. 76) sings *pee-you*. All other *Empidonax* flycatchers have more pronounced eye rings and have characteristic vocalizations: Cordilleran Flycatcher sings *peet seet*; Least Flycatcher sings *che bek*; Hammond's and Dusky flycatchers sing *sillit-tsurp-seet*.

Quick I.D.: sparrow-sized; sexes similar; olive-brown upperparts; no eye ring; two white wing bars; long, narrow, dark tail; dark bill; light throat.
Size: 5–6 in.

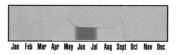

Jan Feb Mar Apr May Jun Jul Aug Sept Oct Nov Dec

Say's Phoebe
Sayornis saya

Launching itself from a sheltered ledge in Castlewood State Park, the Say's Phoebe darts quickly out from the cliff face, loops back and alights on a concealed perch. The Say's Phoebe is a flycatcher that has taken to rocky environments. It frequently reuses its nesting sites from year to year, building its nest under a ledge where it is shielded from harsh weather.

This large, handsome flycatcher is a very early spring migrant that appears in mid-March to greet the upcoming season. Its soft brown plumage and apricot belly grant it a subtle beauty, but its habit of flicking its tail while perched is perhaps its most diagnostic trait. The Say's Phoebe is remarkably tolerant of arid conditions, because it is capable of extracting all the water it requires from the insects it eats.

Similar Species: All other flycatchers (pp. 76–80) lack the apricot belly.

Jan Feb Mar Apr May Jun Jul Aug Sept Oct Nov Dec

Quick I.D.: sparrow-sized; sexes similar; apricot belly and undertail coverts; dark tail; brown-gray breast and upperparts; dark head; no eye ring; very faint wing bars.
Size: 7¹/₂ in.

Western Kingbird
Tyrannus verticalis

The tumble-flight courtship display of the Western Kingbird is one of the most entertaining spring scenes in southern Colorado. While twisting and turning, the male flies 60 feet straight up, suddenly stalls, and then tumbles, flips and twists as he falls toward the ground. Western Kingbirds perform this spectacle each spring over undeveloped open grasslands throughout our area. Once pair bonds are formed, the nest is built on a tree, ledge or utility pole, or atop an abandoned nest. The female lays three to five eggs.

Western Kingbirds are commonly seen perched on fenceposts, barbed wire and power lines, surveying for prey, for much of their time in Colorado. Once prey is sighted, kingbirds may persistently chase the flying insects for up to 40 feet before the bird snaps its bill upon its meal.

Similar Species: None.

Quick I.D.: smaller than a robin; sexes similar; yellow belly; light gray head and throat; dark wings and tail; white outer tail feathers.
Size: 9 in.

Jan Feb Mar Apr May Jun Jul Aug Sept Oct Nov Dec

Eastern Kingbird
Tyrannus tyrannus

When one thinks of a tyrant, images of a large carnivorous dinosaur or a menacing ruler are much more likely to come to mind than the image of a little bird. Although the Eastern Kingbird may not initially seem to be as imposing as other known tyrants, this flycatcher certainly lives up to its scientific name, *Tyrannus tyrannus*. The Eastern Kingbird is pugnacious: it will fearlessly attack crows, hawks, other large birds and even humans that pass through its territory. The intruders are often vigorously pursued, pecked and plucked for some distance, until the kingbird is satisfied that there is no further threat.

The courtship flight of the Eastern Kingbird, which can be seen in fields and shrubby areas, is characterized by short, quivering wing beats— a touching display, even for this little tyrant.

Similar Species: All other flycatchers (pp. 76–79) and Tree Swallow (p. 82) lack the white, terminal tail band and are not black and white.

Jan Feb Mar Apr May Jun Jul Aug Sept Oct Nov Dec

Quick I.D.: smaller than a robin, sexes similar; black head, back, wings and tail; white underneath; white, terminal tail band; orange-red crown (rarely seen). **Size:** 9 in.

White-throated Swift
Aeronautes saxatalis

The White-throated Swift is one of the frequent fliers of the bird world. Only incubation and rest keep this bird out of the air. White-throated Swifts feed, drink, bathe and even mate while flying. During their lifespan, it is likely that many of these birds travel more than a million miles.

The White-throated Swift is a summer resident in our area, and it is commonly seen at Castlewood State Park. These high-flying aeronauts often forage for flying insects at great heights, and they are often visible only as specks in the sky. They have complete mastery of the skies and leisurely forage even at these great heights. This swift nests on vertical crevices, which in the Denver area include cliffs, horizontal cracks, buildings and overpasses.

Similar Species: Chimney Swift lacks the white and dark underparts. Bank Swallow (p. 83) and Violet-green Swallow lack the dark flanks with white patches and the 'wing pits.'

Quick I.D.: sparrow-sized; sexes similar; black upperparts; white throat tapering to belly; black flanks with white patches; slender, sleek body. *In flight:* long, tapering wings angle backward; slightly forked tail.
Size: 6–7 in.

Jan Feb Mar Apr May Jun Jul Aug Sept Oct Nov Dec

Tree Swallow
Tachycineta bicolor

Depending on food availability, Tree Swallows might forage over great distances, darting above open fields and wetlands as they catch flying insects in their bills. These bicolored birds occasionally sweep down to the water surface for a quick drink and a bath. In bad weather, Tree Swallows might fly up to five miles to distant marshes or lakes to find flying insects.

The Tree Swallow is among the first migrants to arrive in the Denver area, often beating the onset of spring weather. It returns to Chatfield Reservoir and most other freshwater marshes in late March to begin its reproductive cycle. It nests in abandoned woodpecker cavities as well as in nest boxes. The cavity is lined with weeds, grasses and long feathers. When the parents leave the eggs for long periods of time, they cover them with feathers. After the young birds hatch, they leave the cavity within three weeks to begin their aerial lives.

Similar Species: Violet-green Swallow is the most similar, but it has white cheeks and white rump sides. Chimney Swift has slimmer wings and a darker belly. Bank Swallow (p. 83) and Northern Rough-winged Swallow lack the blue-green upperparts.

Quick I.D.: sparrow-sized; sexes similar; iridescent blue-green plumage; white underparts; dark rump; small bill; long, pointed wings; shallowly forked tail; small feet.
Size: 5–6 in.

Jan Feb Mar Apr May Jun Jul Aug Sept Oct Nov Dec

Bank Swallow
Riparia riparia

Bank Swallows cruise over wetlands, fields and meadows at low altitudes, catching flying insects gracefully in flight. They often catch transforming insects just as they are emerging from the water to enter their adult stage.

Bank Swallows begin nesting in May. As their name suggests, they choose dirt banks in which to build their nest cavities. These small birds diligently excavate the burrow, first with their small bills and later with their feet. Incredibly, Bank Swallows have been known to kick and scratch out a burrow five feet long, but the typical length is two to three feet. An active Bank Swallow colony is difficult to approach undetected, because the frightened birds launch themselves from their burrows and circle overhead until the threat passes.

Similar Species: Tree Swallow (p. 82) has green or blue upperparts. Northern Rough-winged Swallow lacks the dark chest band.

Quick I.D.: sparrow-sized; sexes similar; brown upperparts; light underparts; dark band on chest; long, pointed wings; small bill; dark cheek; dark rump; small legs.
Size: 5–6 in.

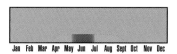

Jan Feb Mar Apr May Jun Jul Aug Sept Oct Nov Dec

SWIFTS & SWALLOWS 83

Barn Swallow
Hirundo rustica

The graceful flight of this bird is a common summer sight. The Barn Swallow often forages at low altitudes, so its deeply forked tail is easily observed. It is actually the only swallow in Denver to have a 'swallow-tail.' The name 'swallow' originated in Europe (it comes from the Old Norse *svala*), where the Barn Swallow is also common and where it is simply called the Swallow. (The verb 'to swallow' comes from the Old Norse *svelgr,* 'a whirlpool.')

The Barn Swallow builds its cup-shaped mud nest in the eaves of barns and picnic shelters, or in any other structure that provides protection from the rain. Because the Barn Swallow is often closely associated with human structures, it is not uncommon for a nervous parent bird to dive repeatedly at human 'intruders,' encouraging them to retreat.

Similar Species: No other swallow has a deeply forked tail. Cliff Swallow (p. 85) is the most similar in coloration.

Quick I.D.: larger than a sparrow; sexes similar, but female is a bit duller; deeply forked tail; glossy blue back, wings and tail; chestnut or buffy underparts; russet throat and forehead.
Size: 6–8 in.

Jan Feb Mar Apr May Jun Jul Aug Sept Oct Nov Dec

Cliff Swallow

Petrochelidon pyrrhonota

The Cliff Swallow is very widespread in Denver, and you can often encounter it in its nesting colonies. Cliff Swallows nest under many of the bridges that span our waters, and clouds of them will sometimes whip up on either side of a bridge. They do not restrict their nesting to bridges, however, and colonies are occasionally found under piers and on abandoned buildings and dry, rocky cliffs.

If you stop to inspect the undersides of a bridge, you may see hundreds of gourd-shaped nests stuck to the pillars and structural beams. The nests are meticulously made from mud, one mouthful at a time. As they busily build their nests, Cliff Swallows create a chaotic scene with their constant procession back and forth between nest and mudflat.

Similar Species: Tree Swallow (p. 82) has a blue-green back. Barn Swallow (p. 84) has a deeply forked tail and a dark rump.

Quick I.D.: sparrow-sized; sexes similar; pale forehead; buff rump; dark back with white stripes; gray-brown wings and tail; white underparts; rusty cheek; dark bib; square tail.
Size: 5–6 in.

Jan Feb Mar Apr May Jun Jul Aug Sept Oct Nov Dec

Steller's Jay
Cyanocitta stelleri

Although scarce within the Denver city limits, the Steller's Jay is present throughout the year in coniferous forests elsewhere around our area. With a crest unmatched by any other North American songbird and delicate blue hues sparkling in its plumage, this bird is as striking as it is extroverted and mischievous. The Steller's Jay is less known to most North Americans than the familiar Blue Jay, and eastern birdwatchers often visit Colorado to sight one.

Steller's Jays travel in loose flocks in August and September, and it is interesting to watch them fly directly to their destination in single-file. These jays noisily announce their arrival with their *shack-shack-shack* calls. The diet of this jay is diverse: it will eat seeds, dog food and insects, and it will scavenge carcasses.

Similar Species: Western Scrub-Jay (p. 87) lacks a crest. Blue Jay has white and black in its plumage.

Jan Feb Mar Apr May Jun Jul Aug Sept Oct Nov Dec

Quick I.D.: larger than a robin; sexes similar; dark crest; blue back, wings and tail; black head; white specks on forehead. **Size:** 11 in.

Western Scrub-Jay

Aphelocoma californica

The Western Scrub-Jay is a jay of open forests, especially scrub and oak woodlands. You may see (and hear) the scrub-jay foraging in its characteristic manner: it frequently buries acorns by pounding them into soft soil and covering them with leaf litter or small stones. Many of the acorns are never retrieved, making scrub-jays effective dispersers for oak trees.

The Western Scrub-Jay is one of the few birds able to eat hairy caterpillars. These caterpillars' guard hairs are an effective defense mechanism because they irritate the digestive tracts of most birds. The scrub-jay rubs the caterpillar down in sand or soil before eating it, however, effectively 'shaving' off the irritating hairs. Scrub-jays also eat spiders, beetles, wasps, termites, nuts, corn, fruit, lizards and small rodents, and they visit feeders stocked with sunflower seeds, suet and peanuts.

Similar Species: Steller's Jay (p. 86) has a crest, a dark blue body and a black hood.

Quick I.D.: larger than a robin; sexes similar; blue head, back and tail; white throat; gray belly; long tail; no crest.
Size: 11–13 in.

Jan	Feb	Mar	Apr	May	Jun	Jul	Aug	Sept	Oct	Nov	Dec

Black-billed Magpie
Pica pica

The beauty of this bird is too often overlooked because its raucous and aggressive demeanor overshadows its gorgeous panda-like plumage. The long, shiny tail of the Black-billed Magpie is one of the longest of any North American bird, and its dark plumage reflects a surprising spectrum of colors from the sun.

Magpies are some of the most exceptional architects that live in the Denver area. The elaborate nest that these birds construct is often found in a spruce tree, but a deciduous tree or an iron bridge can also serve their purpose. Constructed of branches and held together with mud, the domed compartment conceals and protects the eggs and young from harsh weather and predation. It is so well constructed that abandoned nests remain in trees for years, and they are often reused by non–nest builders, such as owls.

Although the wonderfully adaptable magpie might create an annoyance at times with its loud voice and aggressive tactics, it adds a flavor to our cities and rural areas that is distinct and noteworthy.

Similar Species: None.

Jan Feb Mar Apr May Jun Jul Aug Sept Oct Nov Dec

Quick I.D.: smaller than a crow; sexes similar; long, black tail; black head, breast and back; rounded, black and white wings; black undertail coverts; black bill; white belly.
Size: 18–22 in.

American Crow

Corvus brachyrhynchos

The American Crow calls with the classic, long, descending *caaaw*. Every day of the year, this common bird announces the start of the day to Denver residents. In late summer and fall, when their reproductive duties are completed, crows group together to roost in flocks known as 'murders.' The crow population has exploded in our area in recent years, and large flocks can be seen almost anywhere in the Denver area.

This large, black bird's intelligence has led it into many confrontations with humans, from which it often emerges the victor. Scientific studies have shown that crows are capable of solving simple problems, which comes as no surprise to anyone who has watched crows as they snip open garbage bags with scissor-like precision.

Similar Species: Common Raven (p. 90) is larger and has a diamond-shaped tail and a heavier bill.

Quick I.D.: small gull–sized; sexes similar; black; fan-shaped tail; slim overall.
Size: 18–20 in.

Jan Feb Mar Apr May Jun Jul Aug Sept Oct Nov Dec

Common Raven
Corvus corax

Common Ravens are often seen gliding effortlessly on updrafts in the Denver area, offering their hoarse voices to the frosty air. Their deep *quorks*, among a multitude of variations, demostrate a complexity in language and behavior poorly understood even by the most dedicated scientist. The intricacies of this bird's lifestyle make it exceptionally difficult to study scientifically, but these same mysterious traits make even passive naturalists believe that ravens are indeed more complex and evolved than we normally accept.

Whether stealing food from a flock of gulls, harassing an eagle in mid-air, dining from a carcass or confidently strutting among campers at a favorite park, the raven is worthy of its reputation as a clever bird. Glorified in traditional cultures worldwide, ravens are not restricted to the instinctive behaviors of most other birds. With the ability to express themselves playfully—tumbling aimlessly through the air or sliding down a snowy bank on their backs—these large, raucous birds flaunt traits many think of as exclusively human.

Similar Species: American Crow (p. 89) is much smaller and has a fan-shaped tail. Hawks (pp. 43–47) have fan-shaped tails and are not completely black.

Quick I.D.: larger than a hawk; sexes similar; black; large bill; diamond-shaped tail; shaggy throat. *In flight:* spread primaries.
Size: 22–24 in. (male slightly larger).

Jan Feb Mar Apr May Jun Jul Aug Sept Oct Nov Dec

Black-capped Chickadee
Poecile atricapillus

The Black-capped Chickadee is one of the most pleasant birds in urban and forested areas, often seeming to come out and greet walkers along trails. It is a common sight in Denver and can be found in every park and in most landscaped backyards. Throughout most of the year, chickadees move about in loose flocks, investigating nooks and crannies for food and uttering their delicate *chick-a-dee-dee-dee* calls.

During spring, Black-capped Chickadees seem strangely absent from city parks and wooded ravines because they remain inconspicuous while nesting. Once the first fall chill arrives, however, the woods are once again vibrant with their busy activities.

Similar Species: White-breasted Nuthatch (p. 92) lacks the black chin and has a short tail and red undertail coverts. Mountain Chickadee has a white eyebrow and is common in the mountains west of Denver and in Denver itself some winters.

Quick I.D.: smaller than a sparrow; sexes similar; black cap and bib; white cheek; grayish back, wings and tail; light underneath.
Size: 5–6 in.

Jan Feb Mar Apr May Jun Jul Aug Sept Oct Nov Dec

White-breasted Nuthatch
Sitta carolinensis

♂

The White-breasted Nuthatch is a curious bird. To the novice birdwatcher, seeing a nuthatch call repeatedly while clinging to the underside of a branch is an odd sight. To nuthatches, however, this gravity-defying act is as natural as flight is to other birds. In mid-descent, nuthatches frequently pause, arch their heads out at right angles to the trunk and give their distinctive and often repeated nasal *anh-anh-anh-anh* calls. They make their seemingly dangerous headfirst hops appear routine.

White-breasted Nuthatches frequently visit backyard feeders. They seem less at home on the level platform feeders, where they cast aside their tree-trunk talent for a cautious meal of sunflower seeds.

Similar Species: Pygmy Nuthatch (p. 93) is smaller, has a gray head and lacks the red undertail coverts. Red-breasted Nuthatch (common in Denver some years) has a white eyebrow. Black-capped Chickadee (p. 91) has a black bib and a longer tail.

Quick I.D.: sparrow-sized. *Male:* black cap; white cheek and breast; steel-blue back, wings and tail; straight bill; short tail; russet undertail coverts. *Female:* similar, but with a grayish cap.
Size: 6 in.

Jan Feb Mar Apr May Jun Jul Aug Sept Oct Nov Dec

Pygmy Nuthatch
Sitta pygmaea

The Pygmy Nuthatch is one of the most energetic residents in our area forests: it hops continuously up and down trunks and treetops, incessantly probing and calling its high-pitched *te-dee te-dee.* Unlike other birds that forage on tree trunks, nuthatches routinely work their way down trees headfirst. Because of their unusual approach, nuthatches are able to find seeds and invertebrates that woodpeckers and creepers miss.

The Pygmy Nuthatch is quite gregarious, and it often appears in small flocks that increase in size during fall and winter. During winter nights, the Pygmy Nuthatch retreats to communal roosts in cavities where many birds can snuggle together to conserve heat.

Similar Species: White-breasted Nuthatch (p. 92) is larger, has white completely surrounding the eyes, has a black crown and has reddish or rusty undertail coverts. Red-breasted Nuthatch has a white eyebrow and reddish underparts.

Quick I.D.: smaller than a sparrow; sexes similar; brownish cap bordered by dark eye line; white cheek and throat; gray-blue back; short tail; buff-colored underparts; straight bill.
Size: 4–4¹/₂ in.

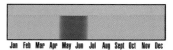

Jan Feb Mar Apr May Jun Jul Aug Sept Oct Nov Dec

Rock Wren
Salpinctes obsoletus

If you scan the rocky outcrops and cliffs at Castlewood State Park, a small rock may suddenly appear to move. This is no visual illusion; rather it is a Rock Wren, a small, gray bird that chooses this stark and barren landscape in which to breed. Like all wrens, Rock Wrens move secretly. They never seem to flush directly in front; rather they appear to sneak away from the corner of your eye.

Rock Wrens are well suited to their chosen homes. They have the most unusual habit of 'paving' the way up to their nests, laying anywhere from 2 to 1500 pebbles as a doormat. Additonally, Rock Wrens have a rather flattened body; they are able to compress themselves to squeeze into crevices and cracks to avoid the blistering midday heat. Rock Wrens are most easily spotted during the cooler hours around dawn and dusk, as they probe the ground and pick under and around rocks with their long, downcurved bill for insects and spiders.

Similar Species: House Wren (p. 95) has brown upperparts and a darker breast. Canyon Wren has a clean white throat, brown underparts and no eyebrow.

Quick I.D.: sparrow-sized; sexes similar; gray-brown upperparts; light underparts; white throat; downcurved bill; finely streaked, white breast; rusty brown rump and tail; tail is trimmed with buff-colored tips.
Size: 5–6 in.

Jan Feb Mar Apr May Jun Jul Aug Sept Oct Nov Dec

House Wren

Troglodytes aedon

This common bird of suburbs, city parks and woodlands sings as though its lungs are bottomless. The sweet, warbling song of the House Wren is distinguished by its melodious tone and its uninterrupted endurance. Although the House Wren is far smaller than a sparrow, it offers an unending song in one breath.

Like all wrens, the House Wren frequently carries its short tail cocked straight up. This bird is often observed in woodlands, city parks and backyards, skulking beneath the dense understorey from May to September. As spring arrives, the House Wren treats Denver neighborhoods to a few weeks of wonderful warbles, and then channels its energy to the task of reproduction.

Similar Species: Winter Wren's tail is shorter than its legs. Rock Wren (p. 94) has a whiter breast.

Quick I.D.: smaller than a sparrow; sexes similar; brown overall; tail is often cocked up; bill is slightly downcurved; tail is as long as legs.
Size: 5 in.

Jan Feb Mar Apr May Jun Jul Aug Sept Oct Nov Dec

Ruby-crowned Kinglet
Regulus calendula

These kinglets are common summer visitors to the coniferous trees in the mountains west of Denver. They move through Denver in spring and fall, continuously flitting through our shrubs. Kinglets always seem to be nervous: their tails and wings flick continuously as they hop from branch to branch in search of grubs and insect eggs.

The Ruby-crowned Kinglet is similar to the Golden-crowned Kinglet in size, habits and coloration, but it has a hidden ruby crown. 'Rubies' are heard more often then they are seen, especially as spring approaches. Their distinctive song starts like a motor chugging to life, and then the kinglets fire off a series of loud, rising *chewy-chewy-chewy-cheewee*. These final, excitable phrases are often the only recognizable part of the song.

Similar Species: Golden-crowned Kinglet has a black outline to its orange crown.

Quick I.D.: smaller than a sparrow; plump; dark olive; white wing bars; dark tail and wings; eye ring. *Male:* red crown (infrequently seen). *Female:* no red crown.
Size: 4 in.

Jan Feb Mar Apr May Jun Jul Aug Sept Oct Nov Dec

Mountain Bluebird
Sialia currucoides

The male Mountain Bluebird is like a piece of sky come to life. Just as the last spring snows are retreating from our area, Mountain Bluebirds arrive from the south. These spring migrations routinely consist of small groups of birds, but, on occasion, Mountain Bluebirds migrate in flocks of more than 100 birds. Because of their early spring arrival, late spring snowstorms occasionally prove fatal for many of these powdery blue blessings.

Mountain Bluebirds can be observed quite easily in open areas, such as in Mt. Falcon County Park, in the foothills west of Denver. Natural nest sites (abandoned woodpecker cavities) are in high demand, and aggressive starlings often usurp bluebirds from these vacancies. As a result, bluebirds now turn to artificial nest boxes, which have been established in many parts of the Denver area. Mountain Bluebirds are becoming increasingly common, and the vigilance of caring residents is rewarded with the sight of a male as he establishes his territory one crisp spring morning.

Similar Species: Male Western Bluebird has a chestnut red breast. Townsend's Solitaire (p. 98) has peach-colored patches in the wings and white outer tail feathers. Western Scrub-Jay (p. 87) is larger and has a longer tail and less intense blue plumage. Steller's Jay (p. 86) and Blue Jay have prominent crests.

Quick I.D.: smaller than a robin; black eyes, bill and legs. *Male:* sky-blue body; upperparts are darker than underparts. *Female:* sky-blue wings, tail and rump; blue-gray back and head; gray underparts. **Size:** 6–7 in.

Jan Feb Mar Apr May Jun Jul Aug Sept Oct Nov Dec

Townsend's Solitaire
Myadestes townsendi

This slim thrush is frequently observed in the mountains, perched on an exposed limb as it surveys the area for food. Townsend's Solitaires flutter out from their viewpoints to catch insects in mid-air or follow them to the ground and grasp them with a soft pounce. In flight, the warm peachy wing linings of this western speciality shine through the wings like early morning sunlight through a bedroom window.

During much of the year, these birds are infrequently seen in groups, and this solitary tendency is well represented in the name. During winter, they descend into our area in greater numbers, claiming berry trees and junipers as their own and defending them against others of their kind. Because insects are scarce during the coldest months of the year, their diet shifts to fruits, which they nimbly pluck off the stems and swallow in one sudden motion.

Similar Species: Female Mountain Bluebird (p. 97) has bluish wings and lacks the peach-colored wing patches and the white outer tail feathers. Northern Mockingbird (p. 114) has lighter underparts and lacks the peach-colored wing patches and the eye ring. Gray Catbird has a black cap and red undertail coverts and lacks the eye ring and the white outer tail feathers.

Quick I.D.: smaller than a robin; sexes similar. *Adult:* gray body; darker wings and tail; peach-colored wing patches (very evident in flight); white eye ring; white outer tail feathers; long tail. *Immature:* brown body is heavily spotted with buff; pale eye ring.
Size: 8–9 in.

Jan Feb Mar Apr May Jun Jul Aug Sept Oct Nov Dec

Swainson's Thrush
Catharus ustulatus

Beauty in forest birds is often gauged by sound, not appearance. Given this criterion, the Swainson's Thrush is certainly one of the most enchanting birds to inhabit Rocky Mountain riparian forests. Swainson's Thrushes are heard but rarely seen during their summer stay, and they reveal themselves to birders mainly when they flock together in migration.

May in the forests of Golden Gate Canyon State Park can prove quite rewarding, because it is common to briefly glimpse these birds as they retreat into the understorey. Visually, Swainson's Thrushes hold no mystery—their olive backs and faintly golden cheeks are not highlighted against the shady backdrop—but the Swainson's Thrush is not about looks, and when its ascending notes meet your ear, the sweet songs crowd out lesser songs, and the thrush's solo reigns.

Similar Species: Hermit Thrush (p. 100) has a reddish rump and tail and gray cheeks, and it often flicks its wings nervously.

Quick I.D.: smaller than a robin; sexes similar; bold, buffy eye ring; golden cheek; lightly spotted throat and breast; white belly and undertail coverts; olive-gray flanks; light underparts.
Size: 6¹/₂–7¹/₂ in.

Jan Feb Mar Apr May Jun Jul Aug Sept Oct Nov Dec

Hermit Thrush
Catharus guttatus

The Hermit Thrush is one of the most beautiful songsters to inhabit Rocky Mountain woodlands and forest floors. Its enchanting song is heard from shady coniferous forests where the understorey is scattered with shrubby nesting cover. The Hermit Thrush is confined to deep forests, such as in Golden Gate Canyon State Park, where its ethereal song sanctifies the groves.

The Hermit Thrush's song lifts the soul with each note and leaves a fortunate listener breathless at its conclusion. The inspiring song is heard early on spring mornings, and the Hermit Thrush is routinely the last of the daytime singers to be silenced by the night. Its song is most appreciated at dusk, when it alone (or perhaps accompanied by a Swainson's Thrush) offers an emotional melody to the darkening forest.

Similar Species: Swainson's Thrush (p. 99) has a prominent, buff eye ring, a golden-brown cheek and an olive brown back and tail.

Jan Feb Mar Apr May Jun Jul Aug Sept Oct Nov Dec

Quick I.D.: smaller than a robin; sexes similar; pale white eye ring; reddish-brown rump and tail; lightly spotted throat and breast; white belly and undertail coverts; gray flanks.
Size: 7–8 in.

American Robin
Turdus migratorius

If not for its abundance, the American Robin's voice and plumage would inspire pause and praise from casual onlookers. Acclimatization has dealt the robin an unsung hand, however, and it is generally not fully appreciated for the pleasures it offers the eyes and ears of Denver-area residents. Nevertheless, the American Robin's close relationship with urban areas has allowed many residents an insight into a bird's life. A robin dashing around a yard in search of worms or ripe berries is as familiar to many people as its three-part *cheerily-cheery up-cheerio* song. American Robins also make up part of the emotional landscape of communities: their lively song, their spotted young and occasionally even their deaths are experiences shared by their human neighbors.

American Robins seem to be year-round residents in Denver, but the bird dashing on your lawn in June might not be the same bird that shivers in February. Unnoticed by most residents, the neighborhood robins take seasonal shifts: new birds arrive from the north and from the mountains just when some summer residents depart for southern climes in fall.

Similar Species: Immature robins can be confused with other thrushes, but robins always have at least a hint of red in the breast.

♂

♀

Quick I.D.: smaller than a jay; dark head, back and tail; yellow bill; striped throat; white undertail coverts. *Male:* brick-red breast; darker hood. *Female:* slightly more orange breast; lighter hood.
Size: 9–11 in.

Jan Feb Mar Apr May Jun Jul Aug Sept Oct Nov Dec

Plumbeous Vireo
Vireo plumbeus

The distinctive 'spectacles' of the Plumbeous Vireo frame the bird's eyes and identify this songbird as it forages purposefully along branches for insects. The white 'frames' are among the boldest of eye rings belonging to songbirds.

During courtship, male Plumbeous Vireos fluff out their yellow flanks and bob ceremoniously to their prospective mates. The slow, high-pitched *look up...see me...here I am* song is rich in quality, and it is commonly heard in our area.

When it comes to building a nest, all vireos tend to share the same floorplan. A horizontal fork in a tree is chosen, and a hanging, basket-like cup nest is made with grass, roots and spider's silk. These characteristic nests are usually quite easy to spot once the leaves have fallen from the trees and the birds have departed to the south.

Until recently, taxonomists grouped the Plumbeous Vireo together with the Cassin's Vireo and the Blue-headed Vireo as a single species, the Solitary Vireo.

Similar Species: Warbling Vireo (p. 103) and Red-eyed Vireo both lack the white 'spectacles.'

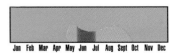

Jan Feb Mar Apr May Jun Jul Aug Sept Oct Nov Dec

Quick I.D.: sparrow-sized; sexes similar; white 'spectacles'; two white wing bars; gray head and upperparts; white underparts; gray flanks; dark tail; stout bill; dark legs.
Size: 5–6 in.

Warbling Vireo
Vireo gilvus

breeding

The Warbling Vireo can be quite common during the summer months, but you still need to make a prolonged search before spotting this bird. Lacking any splashy field marks, the Warbling Vireo is exceedingly difficult to spot unless it moves. Searching the treetops for this inconspicuous bird may be a literal 'pain in the neck,' but the satisfaction in visually confirming its identity can be rewarding.

The velvety voice of the Warbling Vireo contrasts sharply with its dull, nondescript plumage. The often-repeated *I love you, I love you, I love you Ma'am!* song delights the listening forest with its oscillating quality. The phrases finish on an upbeat, as if the bird is asking a question of the wilds.

Similar Species: Red-eyed Vireo has a black-and-white eyebrow and a gray cap.

Quick I.D.: smaller than a sparrow; sexes similar; dull white eyebrow; no wing bars; olive-gray upperparts; greenish flanks; light underparts; gray crown.
Size: 4¹/₂–5¹/₂ in.

Jan Feb Mar Apr May Jun Jul Aug Sept Oct Nov Dec

Virginia's Warbler
Vermivora virginiae

In the foothills of Colorado, the Virginia's Warbler favors dense thickets and shrubs—usually scrub oak or mountain mahogany— to nest and forage. It is often difficult to get a satisfying look at this nervous bird as it twitches and flicks its way through the dense vegetation. This small dainty bird is often best known from its voice, a simple trill of a song, or more commonly a surprisingly ill-placed and harsh *tsick* call note.

The Virginia's Warbler is a classic tail wagger, and it is this feature that is easier to recognize when the bird exposes itself to a viewer. Its foraging movements are easily followed, because this bird takes insects from foliage usually no more than 15 feet from the ground. Its interesting name does not represent one of our eastern states, but rather a simple love. After army surgeon William Wallace Anderson collected the first specimen, he sent it to the Smithsonian Museum and requested that it be named after his wife Virginia.

Similar Species: Nashville Warbler has more yellow on the underparts, especially the throat, and lacks the yellow rump.

breeding

Quick I.D.: smaller than a sparrow. *Male:* gray head and back; yellow breast; white throat; white belly; yellow undertail coverts; white eye ring; yellow-green rump; faint reddish crown patch. *Female:* duller overall.
Size: 4–4¹/₂ in.

Jan Feb Mar Apr May Jun Jul Aug Sept Oct Nov Dec

Yellow Warbler
Dendroica petechia

The Yellow Warbler is common in shrublands and in groves of aspen, willow and cottonwood. As a consequence of its abundance, it is usually the first warbler that birdwatchers identify in their lives—and every spring thereafter. From mid-May through August, this brilliantly colored warbler is easily found in appropriate habitat throughout our area.

During our winters, Yellow Warblers migrate to the tropics, spending September to April in Mexico and South America. Following the first warm days of spring, the first of the Yellow Warblers return. Their distinctive courtship song *sweet-sweet-sweet I'm so-so sweet* is easily recognized in early May despite the eight-month absence. In true warbler fashion, the summertime activities of the Yellow Warbler are energetic and inquisitive, flitting from branch to branch in search of juicy caterpillars, aphids and beetles.

Similar Species: Wilson's Warbler (p. 108) has a small, black cap.

breeding

Quick I.D.: smaller than a sparrow; yellow overall; darker back, wings and tail; dark eyes and bill. *Male:* bold red streaking on breast. *Female:* often lacks red streaking.
Size: 4–5 in.

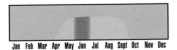

Jan Feb Mar Apr May Jun Jul Aug Sept Oct Nov Dec

Yellow-rumped Warbler
Dendroica coronata

♀

♂

breeding

This spirited songbird is as common as it is delightful. Its contrasting colors, its curiosity and its tinkling trill are enthusiastically admired by even the most jaded birdwatcher. Yellow-rumped Warblers are the only year-round warbler in the Denver area: a few hardy individuals remain to feed on berries and backyard feeders throughout winter. It is not during the coldest months, however, that Yellow-rumps are most noticeable, rather it is during late April, when trees along the Highline Canal come alive with these colorful birds.

The locally breeding race of the Yellow-rumped Warbler has a glorious yellow throat. It was formerly called the Audubon's Warbler, distinguishing it from the white-throated eastern form, which was known as the Myrtle Warbler and which is common in our area during migration and is often here throughout winter. Ironically, although the western race bore the name of one of the greatest ornithologists, it is one of the few birds that Audubon failed to meet in the wild. Although it no longer officially holds the Audubon title, many western birders continue to refer to this spry bird by its former name, affirming its western roots and superior looks.

Similar Species: Eastern Yellow-rumped Warbler (Myrtle Warbler) has a white throat and smaller white wing bars.

Quick I.D.: small sparrow–sized; yellow rump, shoulder patches, crown and throat; blue-black head, back, tail and wings; white wing bars; dark chest band; white belly. *Male:* bright colors. *Female:* less intense colors.

Size: 5–6 in.

Jan Feb Mar Apr May Jun Jul Aug Sept Oct Nov Dec

Common Yellowthroat
Geothlypis trichas

♀

♂

breeding

With so much diversity in North America's wood warbler clan, it is no surprise that at least one species has forsaken forests in favor of cattail marshes. In our area, this energetic warbler reaches its highest abundance along the wetland brambles and cattails near Highline Canal and Barr Lake, but it can be seen and heard along the vegetation bordering many freshwater bodies.

The male Common Yellowthroat is easily identified by his black mask or by his oscillating *witchety-witchety-witchety* song. Female yellowthroats are rarely seen because they keep to their nests deep within the thick vegetation surrounding marshes. The three to five young yellowthroats hatch after only about 12 days of incubation. They develop rapidly, soon leaving the nest and allowing the parents to repeat the process once again. Common Yellowthroat nests are often parasitized by Brown-headed Cowbirds.

Similar Species: Male is distinct. Virginia's Warbler (p. 104) has dark brown legs, a gray back and an eye ring.

Quick I.D.: smaller than a sparrow; orange legs; yellow throat and underparts; olive upperparts. *Male:* black mask, with white border on forehead. *Female:* no mask.
Size: 4¹/₂–5¹/₂ in.

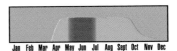

Jan Feb Mar Apr May Jun Jul Aug Sept Oct Nov Dec

Wilson's Warbler
Wilsonia pusilla

The descending trill of the Wilson's Warbler reveals the presence of this small, colorful bird. In classic warbler style, it feeds on caterpillars and other insects in branches that are low to the ground, often near water. Often flitting to within a branch of onlookers, this energetic warbler bounces from one perch to another like an overwound wind-up toy.

This warbler was named for Alexander Wilson, the 'father' of American ornithology. During its spring and fall migrations, the Wilson's Warbler can be found almost anywhere in Denver, including well-planted back-yards. During the nesting season, however, it moves to higher elevations, where it cautiously conceals its nest site.

Similar Species: Male Yellow Warbler (p. 105) has a streaked breast and lacks the black cap, and the female is paler green on the wings and tail.

Jan Feb Mar Apr May Jun Jul Aug Sept Oct Nov Dec

Quick I.D.: smaller than a sparrow; lemon yellow underparts; olive to dark green upperparts. *Male:* black cap. *Female:* duller cap; faint yellow eyebrow.
Size: 4–5 in.

Yellow-breasted Chat
Icteria virens

♂

At nearly eight inches long, the Yellow-breasted Chat is quite literally a warbler and a half. It behaves like a typical warbler, but its curiosity and flitting habits seem misplaced in so large a bird. The Yellow-breasted Chat is also one of the most curious of our nesting warblers, popping up out of its tangled habitat in response to pleading squeaks and pishes.

Chats are bizarre birds, and they often attract attention to themselves through strange vocalizations and noisy thrashing in dense undergrowth. Their whistles, *kuk*s and 'laughs' are linked together or alone in no obvious arrangement. 'Chat' is a wonderfully descriptive and imaginative name, and anyone who encounters this bird will certainly leave with a 'chatty' impression of it.

Similar Species: Virginia's Warbler (p. 104) is much smaller and has a white eye ring and a thinner bill.

Quick I.D.: larger than a sparrow; sexes similar; white 'spectacles'; white 'jaw' line; heavy, black bill; yellow breast; white under-tail coverts; olive green upperparts; long tail; gray-black legs.
Size: 7¹/₂ in.

Jan Feb Mar Apr May Jun Jul Aug Sept Oct Nov Dec

Western Tanager
Piranga ludoviciana

The tropical appearance of the Western Tanager's plumage reinforces the link between the forests of Mexico and western North America. A winter resident of Mexico and a breeder in the mountain woods west of Denver, this tanager is vulnerable to deforestation at both extremes of its range.

Western Tanagers can be difficult to see despite their colorful wardrobe, because they tend to sing a robin-like warble—*hurry-hurry-scurry-scurry*—from high up in forest canopies. Because its song has the same quality as a robin's song, the tanager is frequently disregarded as a common woodland voice. Novice birdwatchers should listen for its hiccup-like *pit-a-tik* call as it cascades to the forest floor.

The Western Tanager is one of Denver's most breathtaking birds, and every brief encounter is sure to make one wish that the meeting might have lasted just a little longer.

Similar Species: Bullock's Oriole (p. 134) and Black-headed Grosbeak (p. 140) lack the reddish head colors.

breeding

Jan Feb Mar Apr May Jun Jul Aug Sept Oct Nov Dec

Quick I.D.: larger than a sparrow. *Breeding male:* unmistakable, magnificent yellow body with contrasting black wings and tail; red highlights on head. *Female* and *Non-breeding male:* olive yellow overall.
Size: 6¹/₂–7¹/₂ in.

Horned Lark
Eremophila alpestris

Horned Larks are probably most frequently encountered as they rise up in front of vehicles speeding along country roads. Larks cut off to the side of cars an instant before a fatal collision, briefly showing off their distinct, white outer tail feathers on a black tail. Horned Larks resort to these near misses because their first instinct when threatened is to outrun their pursuer. Cars can easily overtake these swift runners, so they take to the air when their first attempt to flee fails.

Late winter is the best season to observe these open country specialists, because they congregate in huge flocks on outlying farm fields, eating waste grain. Most of these birds are destined to migrate north when the first hints of warmth loosen the winter's chilly grip. This does not mean, however, that our area is free of these birds through summer, because many larks nest in our open fields, pastures and mountain tops. They are among the earliest of our courting birds, singing their songs and diving dare-devilishly both before and after one of our spring snowstorms.

Similar Species: Sparrows (pp. 119–26) lack the black facial and throat markings.

♂

Quick I.D.: larger than a sparrow; brown overall; black bib, mask and 'tiara'; light underparts; white outer tail feathers; faint yellow throat. *Female:* duller overall; 'horns' are less prominent.
Size: 7–8 in.

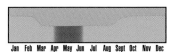

Jan Feb Mar Apr May Jun Jul Aug Sept Oct Nov Dec

European Starling
Sturnus vulgaris

In 1937, 47 years after their intentional release in New York's Central Park, European Starlings began to establish themselves in Colorado. Slightly more than a decade later, flocks of over one million birds were being reported. Today, European Starlings are one of the most common birds in Denver. Their presence is highlighted by astonishing numbers roosting communally during the winter months.

Unfortunately, the expansion of starlings has come at the expense of many of our native birds, including some woodpeckers and the bluebirds, which are unable to defend nest cavities against the aggressive starlings. While few birdwatchers are pleased with the presence of this foreigner to our area, starlings have become a permanent fixture in the bird community. If residents are unable to find joy in this bird's mimicry and flocking, they may take some comfort from the fact that starlings now provide a reliable and stable food source for hawks and the Peregrine Falcon.

Similar Species: All blackbirds (pp. 128 & 130–33) have longer tails and black bills.

breeding

Quick I.D.: smaller than a robin; sexes similar; short tail. *Breeding:* dark, glossy plumage; long, yellow bill. *Non-breeding:* dark bill; spotty plumage. *Juvenile:* brown upperparts; gray-brown underparts; brown bill.
Size: 8–9 in.

Jan Feb Mar Apr May Jun Jul Aug Sept Oct Nov Dec

Loggerhead Shrike
Lanius ludovicianus

Although at first glance a Loggerhead Shrike may look just like a chunky Northern Mockingbird, this similarity is very deceiving. The Loggerhead Shrike is a very special bird in our area: not only are its numbers declining, but also it has behaviors that border on the macabre. Rather than singing to establish territories and attract mates, Loggerhead Shrikes take a rather ghastly approach: they impale prey. All about a male's territory in spring one can find dead carcasses of birds, small mammals, insects and reptiles skewered onto thorns and barbed wire. Although these actions might not appeal to our refined idea of romance, they demonstrate the male's competence to female shrikes.

These 'Butcher Birds' do not limit their impaling to spring: this behavior continues throughout their stay, as a means of storing excess food items during times of plenty. Unless a visit to Chatfield State Park or another open grassland is planned, the Loggerhead Shrike is a bird easily missed during its stay in Denver.

Similar Species: Northern Mockingbird (p. 114) lacks the black mask and has paler, less contrasting wings and tail.

Quick I.D.: robin-sized; sexes similar; black mask; dark gray crown and back; black wings and tail; light gray underparts; hooked bill. *In flight:* white patches in wings and outer tail; quick wing beats. *Immature:* paler and slightly barred upperparts and underparts.
Size: 8–10 in.

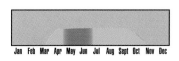

Jan Feb Mar Apr May Jun Jul Aug Sept Oct Nov Dec

Northern Mockingbird
Mimus polyglottos

Once largely restricted to desert scrub in southern Colorado, the Northern Mockingbird is now sometimes seen in Denver during summer. Mockingbirds followed agricultural and urban development northward, and these common urban birds have adapted well to the broken forests and urban fruit-bearing bushes so common in our region.

The Northern Mockingbird is perhaps best known for its ability to mimic sounds. It can expertly imitate other birds, barking dogs and even musical instruments. So accurate is the mimicry, that sonographic analysis often cannot detect differences between the original version and the mockingbird's.

Similar Species: Loggerhead Shrike (p. 113) has a black mask and a stout, hooked bill.

Jan Feb Mar Apr May Jun Jul Aug Sept Oct Nov Dec

Quick I.D.: robin-sized; sexes similar; white patches in black wings; white outer tail feathers; gray head and back; light underparts; long tail; thin bill.
Size: 10–11 in.

Cedar Waxwing
Bombycilla cedrorum

A faint, high-pitched trill is often your first clue that waxwings are around. Search the treetops to see these cinnamon-crested birds as they dart out in quick bursts, snacking on flying insects. Cedar Waxwings are found in many habitats throughout Denver, wherever ripe berries provide abundant food supplies.

Cedar Waxwings are most often seen in large flocks in late fall, when they congregate on fruit trees and quickly eat all the berries. Some people remember these visits not only for the birds' beauty, but because fermentation of the fruit occasionally renders the flock flightless from intoxication.

Similar Species: Bohemian Waxwing, sometimes a common winter visitor, has rufous undertail coverts.

Quick I.D.: smaller than a robin; sexes similar; fine, pale brown plumage; small crest; black mask; yellow belly wash; yellow-tipped tail; light undertail coverts; shiny red (waxy-looking) droplets on wing tips.
Size: 7–8 in.

Jan Feb Mar Apr May Jun Jul Aug Sept Oct Nov Dec

American Dipper
Cinclus mexicanus

The American Dipper may be the world's most unusual songbird. Along fast-flowing mountain waters, it stands bobbing up and down on a streamside rock. In its search for food, a dipper will dive into the water, disappearing momentarily below the stream's surface. Its stout body form, strong claws and thick feathers enable the dipper to survive in cold, fast-flowing water. Regardless of the season, once the bird is well fed, it perches close to the stream and sings its bubbly notes.

America's premier naturalist, John Muir, wrote: 'Find a fall, or cascade, or rushing rapid...and there you will find the complementary Ouzel, flitting about in the spray, diving in foaming eddies, whirling like a leaf among beaten foam-bells; ever vigorous and enthusiastic, yet self-contained, and neither seeking nor shunning your company.' ('Water Ouzel' is an old name for the American Dipper.)

Similar Species: None, although it looks like a large, dark gray wren.

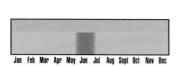

Jan Feb Mar Apr May Jun Jul Aug Sept Oct Nov Dec

Quick I.D.: smaller than a robin; sexes similar; short tail; short neck; flesh-colored legs; stout body. *Adult:* slate gray plumage; head and neck darker than body; straight, black bill. *Immature:* lighter bill; light underparts.
Size: 7–8 in.

Green-tailed Towhee
Pipilo chlorurus

The Green-tailed Towhee is a classic double-scratcher, quickly jumping forward and jumping back again in loose debris in its attempts to uncover insects, seeds and berries. It tends to live out its life under the shade of small shrubs, attracting little attention to itself. A true sparrow, the Green-tailed Towhee prefers to run away from danger, but if it cannot skulk away from threats, it will unwillingly flush, producing an annoyed mewing call.

In migration, Green-tailed Towhees are found in scrub and shrubs around Barr Lake and other arid lands in our region. In these dry communities, their loud springtime courtship chorus carries above the sounds of most of the surrounding birds. These towhees breed in oak scrub west of town and winter mostly south of Colorado.

Similar Species: Chipping Sparrow (p. 120) has a clear white eyebrow and a black eye line and lacks the green back. American Tree Sparrow (p. 119) has a clear-white throat and a black breast spot and lacks the green upperparts.

Quick I.D.: large sparrow; sexes similar.
Adult: rufous crown; 'metallic' green upperparts; white throat outlined in black; sooty gray face and breast; conical, gray bill.
Immature: streaked upperparts; streaked underparts; pale throat outlined in black.
Size: 6¹/₂–7 in.

Jan Feb Mar Apr May Jun Jul Aug Sept Oct Nov Dec

Spotted Towhee
Pipilo maculatus

This large, colorful sparrow is most often heard first as it scratches away leaves and debris in the dense understorey. It is a year-round resident in many parks in the oak-covered foothills west of Denver. It will visit well-stocked feeders during winter, splashing the ground with its colorful plumage.

To best observe this bird, which was formerly grouped with the Eastern Towhee (together they were known as the Rufous-sided Towhee), learn a few birding tricks. Squeaking and pishing are irresistible for towhees, which will quickly pop out from the cover to investigate the curious noise. From deep in the shadows of shrubs, the Spotted Towhee's sharp, nasal *t'wee* call, and its *Here here here PLEASE!* song will also easily identify this boldly colored sparrow.

Similar Species: American Robin (p. 101) is larger and has no white on its chest. Black-headed Grosbeak (p. 140) has an orange chest, a larger bill and a shorter tail. Dark-eyed Junco (p. 127) is smaller and lacks the white spotting on its back.

Quick I.D.: smaller than a robin; black head; rufous-colored flanks; spotted back; white outer tail feathers; white underparts; red eyes. *Male:* black head, breast and upperparts. *Female:* grayish head, breast and upperparts.
Size: 9 in.

Jan Feb Mar Apr May Jun Jul Aug Sept Oct Nov Dec

American Tree Sparrow
Spizella arborea

The American Tree Sparrow's annual flood into Colorado during late fall is a sign of the changing seasons. For the entire winter, these arctic nesters decorate the leafless rural shrublands like ornaments on a Christmas tree. As a regular arrival in late October and one of the first songbirds to disappear in April, the American Tree Sparrow's activities quietly announce the closing of fall and the opening of spring.

These humble, quiet sparrows often go unnoticed despite their large numbers. American Tree Sparrows often visit suburban feeders during their migrations and while wintering in the Denver area, but they never attempt to usurp the surly resident flocks of House Sparrows or House Finches.

Similar Species: Chipping Sparrow (p. 120) lacks the faint breast spot.

non-breeding

Quick I.D.: mid-sized sparrow; sexes similar; red crown; gray eyebrow; small central chest spot (breast is otherwise unstreaked); streaked back.
Size: 6 in.

Jan Feb Mar Apr May Jun Jul Aug Sept Oct Nov Dec

Chipping Sparrow
Spizella passerina

breeding

Hopping around freshly mowed lawns, the cheery Chipping Sparrow goes about its business unconcerned by the busy world of suburban Denver. One of Colorado's most widespread species in migration, the Chipping Sparrow brings birdwatching to those who rarely venture from the city.

These sparrows nest frequently in backyards west of the city, building their small nest cups with dried vegetation and lining them with animal hair. Chipping Sparrows usually attempt to bring off two broods of young every year in Denver. Three or four small, greenish-blue eggs are laid first in mid-May, and again near the beginning of July, should conditions prove favorable. These passive birds are delightful neighbors in our backyards, and they demand nothing more than a little privacy around the rose bush, vine tangle or small tree where they have chosen to nest.

Similar Species: American Tree Sparrow (p. 119) is only a winter resident and has a black, central chest spot. Swamp Sparrow lacks the clean white eyebrow and black eye line.

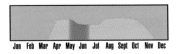

Jan Feb Mar Apr May Jun Jul Aug Sept Oct Nov Dec

Quick I.D.: small sparrow; sexes similar; red crown; white eyebrow; black eye line; clear grayish breast; mottled back.
Size: 5 1/2 in.

Vesper Sparrow

Pooecetes gramineus

In the foothills, which swarm with multitudes of confusing sparrows, the Vesper Sparrow offers birdwatchers a welcome relief: a chestnut patch tucked neatly on the bird's shoulder announces its identity in flight. While perched, its dress is off-the-rack sparrow drab, but its song is simple and customized. This grass-loving bird is one of the lead singers of the foothills chorus. It sings four characteristic, preliminary notes followed by an aimless melody: *here-here there-there, everybody-down-the-hill.*

Vesper Sparrows are common breeders in foothill grasslands west of Denver. They nest in scrapes on the ground, often under a canopy of grass. The small cup nest is woven with grass and lined with finer materials upon which the female incubates four to five eggs for up to 13 days. Although Vesper Sparrows are numerous in our area, nest sites are so secretly placed that their locations are rarely found.

Similar Species: Savannah Sparrow (p. 124) lacks the white outer tail feathers and the chestnut shoulder patch.

Quick I.D.: mid-sized sparrow; sexes similar; weak flank streaking; white outer tail feathers; chestnut shoulder patch; white eye ring; dark upper mandible; lighter lower mandible; light-colored legs.
Size: 5¹/₂–6¹/₂ in.

Jan Feb Mar Apr May Jun Jul Aug Sept Oct Nov Dec

Lark Sparrow
Chondestes grammacus

Good habitat for the Lark Sparrow is easy to spot: the air is dry, the landscape is baked by blazing summer days and the sweet smell of sage soaks the arid flats. There the Lark Sparrow can be observed singing atop short bushes or on rocky ledges, proclaiming itself to its distinctive habitat.

The habitat recipe for Lark Sparrows is fulfilled around Rocky Mountain Arsenal. They arrive before the end of April and sing their songs from the air. Once a pair bond is formed, the birds make a bulky cup nest with grass. The female incubates four to five lightly spotted eggs. Lark Sparrows differ—thankfully for the naturalist—from other prairie-dwelling sparrows: their distinctive red, black and white facial markings and their white outer tail feathers enable even novice bidwatchers to confidently identify these specialists of the sageflats.

Similar Species: No other sparrow has the distinctive head pattern.

Quick I.D.: mid-sized sparrow; sexes similar; distinctive, red-white-and-black 'helmet,' made up of a white throat, eyebrow and crown stripe and a few black lines breaking up an otherwise chestnut-red head; pale, unstreaked breast; central breast spot; black tail with white outer tail feathers; soft brown, mottled back and wings; light-colored legs.
Size: 6 in.

Jan Feb Mar Apr May Jun Jul Aug Sept Oct Nov Dec

Lark Bunting
Calamospiza melanocorys

♂

breeding

At Rocky Mountain Arsenal, where the grasslands have retained their purity, you might be lucky to witness the annual courtship of the Lark Bunting. Like a large butterfly, the male flutters, beating his wings slowly and deeply as he rises high above the flat prairie. His bell-like, tinkling song spreads over the flat landscape until he folds in his wings and floats to the ground like a falling leaf. The courtship behavior of the Lark Bunting, the state bird of Colorado, might be influenced by times long before fenceposts and power poles. Because there were no high points on which to perch on the open prairie, Lark Buntings learned to deliver their songs on the wing.

In spring, the male is a bold beauty, but by the time August arrives his wardrobe has faded to match the year-round subtlety of his mate. During their fall departure, Lark Buntings can pass close by without attracting a glance.

Similar Species: All other sparrows (pp. 117–27) lack the white wing patch. Male Bobolink has a creamy nape, a white rump and white back patches.

Quick I.D.: large sparrow; dark, conical bill. *Breeding male:* all-black plumage; large, white wing and tail-tip patches.
Female: large, white wing patch; mottled gray-brown upperparts; lightly streaked underparts; pale eyebrow.
Size: 7 in.

Jan Feb Mar Apr May Jun Jul Aug Sept Oct Nov Dec

Savannah Sparrow
Passerculus sandwichensis

The Savannah Sparrow is a common bird of the open country. Its dull brown plumage and streaked breast conceal it perfectly in the long grasses of native prairie, farms and roadsides. It breeds in fields of weedy annuals and grasses at Barr Lake State Park.

The Savannah Sparrow resorts to flight only as a last alternative—it prefers to run swiftly and inconspicuously through long grass—and it is most often seen darting across roads and open fields. The Savannah Sparrow's distinctive buzzy trill—*tea-tea-tea-teeea today*—and the yellow patch in front of each eye are the best ways to distinguish it from the many other grassland sparrows.

Similar Species: Vesper Sparrow (p. 121) lacks the yellow lores, has white outer tail feathers and a chestnut shoulder patch.

Quick I.D.: small sparrow; sexes similar; streaked underparts and upperparts; mottled brown above; dark cheek; no white outer tail feathers; many have yellow lores.
Size: 5–6 in.

Jan Feb Mar Apr May Jun Jul Aug Sept Oct Nov Dec

Song Sparrow
Melospiza melodia

The Song Sparrow's drab, heavily streaked plumage doesn't prepare you for its symphonic song, which stands among the best by Denver-area songsters in complexity and rhythm. This commonly heard bird seems to be singing *hip-hip-hip hooray boys, the spring is here again.*

This year-round resident is encountered in a wide variety of habitats: Song Sparrows are easily found in all seasons among marshes, thickets, brambles, weedy fields and woodland edges. Although these birds are most easily identified by their grayish facial streaks while perched, flying birds, which resemble apostrophes, characteristically pump their tails.

Similar Species: Savannah Sparrow (p. 124) and Lincoln's Sparrow have weaker breast streaks.

Quick I.D.: mid-sized sparrow; sexes similar; heavy breast streaks form central chest spot; brown-red plumage; striped head.
Size: 6–7 in.

Jan Feb Mar Apr May Jun Jul Aug Sept Oct Nov Dec

White-crowned Sparrow

Zonotrichia leucophrys

White-crowned Sparrows are usually seen foraging on the ground or in low shrubs. They normally feed a short distance from thickets and tall grasses, always maintaining a quick escape path into the safety of concealing vegetation. Migrating White-crowned Sparrows can often be observed feeding at backyard feeders.

These common summer residents of the Colorado foothills and mountains are among the easiest of the sparrows to identify through looks and voice. From early spring through fall, these boldly patterned sparrows sing *I-I-I-I gotto go wee wee wee now* from the tops of bushes. White-crowns are very persistent singers, and their songs can be heard well into the Rocky Mountain nights.

Similar Species: White-throated Sparrow (uncommon in Denver in fall and winter) has yellow lores and a clear white throat.

Jan Feb Mar Apr May Jun Jul Aug Sept Oct Nov Dec

Quick I.D.: mid-sized sparrow; sexes similar. *Adult:* striped, black-and-white crown; pink bill; unstreaked breast and belly; brown upperparts. *Immature:* striped brown and gray crown; pink bill; brown upperparts; unstreaked breast and belly.
Size: 5¹/₂–7 in.

Dark-eyed Junco

Junco hyemalis

'*Gray-headed Junco*'

♂

The Dark-eyed Junco breeds and lives year-round in the foothills and mountains west of Denver. It is a ground dweller, and it is frequently seen flushing from the undergrowth along wooded trails in Denver's parks. The distinctive, white outer tail feathers flash in alarm as it flies down a narrow path before disappearing into a thicket.

The Dark-eyed Junco's descending trill is easily mistaken for the song of the Chipping Sparrow. The confusion of species can build, because both the Dark-eyed Junco and the Chipping Sparrow occur in similar habitats. A visual identification is usually required to determine the species.

To further confuse the novice naturalist, juncos in Denver come in several different plumages. Our resident birds are 'Gray-headed Juncos,' but 'Slate-colored,' 'Pink-sided,' 'Oregon' and 'White-winged' juncos make yearly appearances in winter. Whatever its appearance, a junco's distinctive smacking call and its habit of double-scratching at forest litter can help identify it. Juncos are frequent guests at bird feeders throughout Denver, usually cleaning up the scraps that have fallen to the ground.

Similar Species: Spotted Towhee (p. 118) is larger and has conspicuous, rufous sides. Brown-headed Cowbird (p. 133) lacks the white outer tail feathers and the white belly.

Quick I.D.: mid-sized sparrow; pale bill; white outer tail feathers. *Male Gray-headed:* gray head and upperparts; reddish brown back. *Male Oregon:* black head; brown back. *Male White-winged:* gray upperparts; white wing bars. *All females:* slightly paler than males.
Size: 5–6½ in.

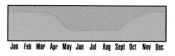

Jan Feb Mar Apr May Jun Jul Aug Sept Oct Nov Dec

Red-winged Blackbird
Agelaius phoeniceus

From March through July, no marsh is free from the loud calls and bossy, aggressive nature of the Red-winged Blackbird. A springtime walk around Barr Lake or through the brush at Cherry Creek State Park will be accompanied by this bird's loud, raspy and persistent *konk-a-reee* or *eat my CHEEEzies* song. During fall migration, the shorelines and farmlands around Denver can become congested with thousands of these birds as they flock their way southward. Many flocks remain through the Denver winter.

The male's bright red shoulders are his most important tool in the intricate displays he uses to defend his territory from rivals and to attract mates. In experiments, males whose red shoulders were painted black soon lost their territories to rivals they had previously defeated. The female's interest lies not in the individual combatants, but in the nesting habitat, and a male who can successfully defend a large area of dense cattails will breed with many females. After the females have built their concealed nests and laid their eggs, the male continues his persistent vigil.

Similar Species: Brewer's Blackbird (p. 131) and Brown-headed Cowbird (p. 133) lack the red shoulder patches.

Quick I.D.: larger than a sparrow. *Male:* all-black plumage; large red patch bordered by creamy yellow on each shoulder. *Female:* brown overall; heavily streaked; hint of red on shoulder. **Size:** 7¹/₂–9¹/₂ in.

Jan Feb Mar Apr May Jun Jul Aug Sept Oct Nov Dec

Western Meadowlark
Sturnella neglecta

Western Meadowlarks are well adapted to the landscape of the fields and pastures where they spend their summers. The song of the Western Meadowlarks signals their arrival in March to territories in open country, such as at Chatfield and Cherry Creek state parks. The superb melody is a trademark of the western prairies that refuses to harmonize with any paraphrase given to it in our language.

Western Meadowlarks are both showy and perfectly camouflaged. Their yellow sweater, with the black V-neck, and white outer tail feathers serve to attract mates. Potential meadowlark mates face one another, raise their bills high and perform a grassland ballet. Oddly, the colorful breast and white tail feathers are also used to attract the attention of potential predators. Foxes, hawks or falcons focus on these bold features in pursuit, but then their prey mysteriously disappears into the grass whenever the meadowlark chooses to turn its back or fold away its white tail flags.

Similar Species: Savannah Sparrow (p. 124) is much smaller and lacks the yellow chest and the white outer tail feathers. Dickcissel is smaller, lacks the white outer tail feathers and is quite uncommon in our area.

Quick I.D.: robin-sized; sexes similar; mottled brown upperparts; black 'V' on chest; yellow throat and belly; white outer tail feathers; striped head.
Size: 8–10 in.

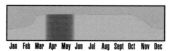

Jan Feb Mar Apr May Jun Jul Aug Sept Oct Nov Dec

Yellow-headed Blackbird

Xanthocephalus xanthocephalus

In a perfect world, male Yellow-headed Blackbirds would have a song to match their splendid plumage. A spring trip to West Quincy Lakes, however, often reveals the unfortunate truth: when the male arches his golden head backward, he struggles to produce a painful, pathetic, metallic grind. Although the song of the Yellow-headed Blackbird might be the worst in North America, its quality soon becomes an appreciated aspect of its marshy home—together with the smell, the insects and the clammy sogginess.

In early spring, before major hatches of insects have risen from the marshes, these blackbirds can be seen curiously probing into the heads of last year's cattails in search of food. Once insects become abundant, Yellow-headed Blackbirds build their nests in loose colonies in cattail marshes and shoreline plants. Their deep, bulky basket nest is usually woven into emergent vegetation over water, and it is made with wet vegetation, which tightens when dry.

Similar Species: Male is distinctive. Female Brewer's Blackbird (p. 131) lacks the yellow throat and face.

Jan Feb Mar Apr May Jun Jul Aug Sept Oct Nov Dec

Quick I.D.: robin-sized. *Male:* yellow head and breast; black back, wings, tail and underparts; white wing patches; black lores; long tail; black bill. *Female:* dusky brown overall; yellow breast, throat and eyebrow; hints of yellow in the face.
Size: 8–11 in.

Brewer's Blackbird

Euphagus cyanocephalus

These small blackbirds are common at Red Rocks Park, where they squabble with pigeons and starlings for leftover scraps of food. In the Denver area, this species is most abundant in rural pastureland, in river valleys and along highways, where they are observed strutting confidently in defiance of nearby, rapidly moving vehicles.

Brewer's Blackbirds are bold, and they allow us to easily and intimately observe them. By studying the behavior of several birds within a flock, you can determine the hierarchy of the flock as it is perceived by the birds themselves. Brewer's Blackbird feathers, which superficially appear black, actually show an iridescent quality as reflected rainbows of sunlight move along the feather shafts.

Similar Species: Male Red-winged Blackbird (p. 128) has a red patch on each wing. Brown-headed Cowbird (p. 133) has a shorter tail and a stout bill, and the male has a brown hood.

Quick I.D.: robin-sized; long tail; slim bill. *Male:* all-black, slightly iridescent plumage; light yellow eyes. *Female:* brown overall; brown eyes.
Size: 8–10 in.

Jan Feb Mar Apr May Jun Jul Aug Sept Oct Nov Dec

Common Grackle
Quiscalus quiscula

The Common Grackle is a noisy and cocky bird that prefers to feed on the ground in open areas. Bird feeders in rural areas can attract large numbers of these blackish birds, whose cranky disposition drives away most other birds (even the quarrelsome jays and House Sparrows). The Common Grackle is easily identified by its long tail, large bill and dark plumage, which may shine with hues of green, purple and blue in bright light.

The Common Grackle is a poor but spirited singer. Usually while perched in a shrub, a male grackle will slowly take a deep breath that inflates his chest and causes his feathers to rise. Then he closes his eyes and gives out a loud, surprising *swaaaack*. Despite our perception of the Common Grackle's musical weakness, following his 'song' the male smugly and proudly poses with his bill held high.

Similar Species: Brown-headed Cowbird (p. 133), American Crow (p. 89) and Brewer's Blackbird (p. 131) all have relatively shorter tails.

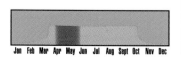

Jan Feb Mar Apr May Jun Jul Aug Sept Oct Nov Dec

Quick I.D.: jay-sized; female is smaller and browner, with a less dramatic tail; glossy black at a distance; faintly iridescent bronze and purple in good light; long tail; large bill. **Size:** 11–13 in.

Brown-headed Cowbird
Molothrus ater

The Brown-headed Cowbird is well established within the matrix of our region's bird life. Historically, this gregarious bird followed the wanderings of bison, and it is now very common in outlying agricultural areas. Cowbirds can be seen in large numbers along Barr Lake during migration.

The Brown-headed Cowbird is infamous for being a nest parasite. Female cowbirds do not incubate their own eggs, but instead lay them in the nests of many songbirds. Cowbird eggs have a short incubation period, and the cowbird chicks often hatch before the host songbird's own chicks. Many songbirds will continue to feed the fast-growing cowbird chick even after it has outgrown its surrogate parent. In its efforts to get as much food as possible, a cowbird chick may squeeze the host's own young out of the nest. The populations of some songbirds have been reduced in part by the activities of the Brown-headed Cowbird, but other songbird species recognize the foreign egg, and they either eject it from their nest or they build a new nest.

Similar Species: Common Grackle (p. 132) has a much longer tail. Brewer's Blackbird (p. 131) has a slimmer body and yellow eyes.

Quick I.D.: larger than a sparrow; dark eyes. *Male:* metallic-looking, glossy black plumage; soft brown head. *Female:* brownish gray overall; slight chest streaks.
Size: 6–8 in.

Jan Feb Mar Apr May Jun Jul Aug Sept Oct Nov Dec

Bullock's Oriole

Icterus bullockii

Although it is a common summer resident of city parks and wooded valleys, the Bullock's Oriole is seldom seen. Unlike the American Robin, which inhabits the human domain of shrubs and lawns, the Bullock's Oriole nests and feeds in the tallest deciduous trees available. This bird's hanging, six-inch-deep, pouch-like nest is deceptively strong, and the vacant nest, which is easily seen on bare trees in fall, is often the only indication that a pair of orioles summered in an area.

From mid-May to mid-July, mature cottonwood trees at Cherry Creek Park are the most productive destinations for oriole-starved Denver-area birdwatchers. The male Bullock's Oriole's striking, Halloween-like, black-and-orange plumage flashes like embers amidst the dense foliage of the treetops, while his song, alternately smooth and harsh, drips to the ground below.

Similar Species: Western Tanager (p. 110) has yellow plumage, a relatively shorter tail and a heavier bill.

Quick I.D.: smaller than a robin.
Male: brilliant orange face, belly, outer tail feathers and rump; black crown, upper back, wings, bib and central tail feathers; large white wing patch; black eye line.
Female: yellow-green upperparts; yellow throat.
Size: 9 in.

Jan Feb Mar Apr May Jun Jul Aug Sept Oct Nov Dec

Gray-crowned Rosy-Finch
Leucosticte tephrocotis

During summer, Gray-crowned Rosy-Finches thrive on alpine tundra, where the air is thin and the wind a frigid fixture. These 'ice-box' breeders nest on the isolated islands of tundra sprinkled along the spine of the Canadian Rockies. During winter, however, Gray-crowned Rosy-Finches spill out of the attic of the Rockies to flock together widely at lower elevations in and around the Denver area. It is at this time of year that the tight flocks of these avian mountaineers are most easily encountered. They routinely hop about in Red Rocks Park, frequently highlighting their fine plumage against a snowy backdrop. Gray-crowned Rosy-Finches occasionally visit feeders in outlying areas, bringing a wilderness quality to the backyards of perceptive residents.

Similar Species: Brown-capped Rosy-Finch, which breeds in the Colorado Rockies (but is less common around Denver in winter than the Gray-crown), lacks the gray crown. Black Rosy-Finch is black where the Gray-crowned is brown.

breeding

Quick I.D.: sparrow-sized; dark bill; black forehead; gray crown; rosy shoulder, rump and belly; brown cheek, back and breast; black legs; dark tail and flight feathers. *Female:* duller overall.
Size: 5¹/₂–6¹/₂ in.

Jan Feb Mar Apr May Jun Jul Aug Sept Oct Nov Dec

House Finch
Carpodacus mexicanus

The House Finch's song is one of the earliest voices to announce the coming of spring. These common city and country birds sing their warbling melodies from backyards, parks, ivy vines and telephone lines.

In the early 1900s, these birds, native to the American Southwest, were popular cage birds, and they were sold across the continent as Hollywood Finches. Elsewhere in the United States, House Finches are recent arrivals, invading eastern cities from intentional releases in the 1920s and 1930s. In Denver, however, their presence is far less intentional: House Finches spread naturally into our area from their southwestern stronghold once much of the landscape was converted to their liking. These wondrous singers add color and complexity to our yards, and they are appreciated guests at winter feeders.

Similar Species: Male Cassin's Finch is raspberry-colored, and the female has a brown cheek contrasting with a white eyebrow and a mustache stripe.

Quick I.D.: sparrow-sized. *Male:* deep red forehead, eyebrow and throat; buffy gray belly; brown cheek; streaked sides and undertail coverts. *Female:* brown overall; streaked underparts; lacks the prominent eyebrow.
Size: 5–6 in.

Jan Feb Mar Apr May Jun Jul Aug Sept Oct Nov Dec

Pine Siskin
Carduelis pinus

Tight, wheeling flocks of these gregarious birds are frequently heard before they are seen. Their characteristic call—*zzzweeet*—starts off slowly and then climbs to a high-pitched climax. Once you recognize this distinctive call, a flurry of activity in the treetops, showing occasional flashes of yellow, will confirm the presence of Pine Siskins.

The Pine Siskin is a year-round, but unpredictable, resident in Denver, and in all seasons it can be found in moist conifer stands in most of the larger parks. Occasionally, flocks descend into weedy fields and shrubby areas, where siskins use their pointed bills to extract the seeds of red alder and thistles in fall. More reliably, flocks of Pine Siskins stake out well-treed neighborhoods and line up at upside-down finch feeders offering niger seed.

Similar Species: Song Sparrow (p. 125), female finches (pp. 135–36) and female crossbills all lack the yellow wing and tail linings.

Quick I.D.: smaller than a sparrow; sexes similar; streaked underparts; yellow flashes in wings and tail; streaked brown upperparts. *Juvenile:* white or creamy wing and tail patches.
Size: 5 in.

Jan Feb Mar Apr May Jun Jul Aug Sept Oct Nov Dec

American Goldfinch
Carduelis tristis

breeding

Throughout the year, the American Goldfinch swings over fields in its distinctive, undulating flight, and it fills the air with its jubilant *po-ta-to chip!* call. This bright, cheery songbird is commonly seen during summer in weedy fields, roadsides and backyards, where it often feeds on thistle seeds. The American Goldfinch delays nesting until June or July to ensure a dependable source of insects, thistles and dandelion seeds to feed its young.

The American Goldfinch is a common backyard bird in parts of the Denver area, and it can easily be attracted to feeding stations that offer a supply of niger (or 'thistle') seed. Unfortunately, goldfinches are easily bullied at feeders by larger sparrows and finches. Only goldfinches and Pine Siskins invert for food, however, so a special finch feeder with openings below the perches is ideal for ensuring a steady stream of these 'wild canaries.'

Similar Species: Yellow Warbler (p. 105) does not have black on the forehead or wings. Evening Grosbeak (p. 139) is much larger and has broad, white wing patches.

Quick I.D.: smaller than a sparrow. *Breeding male:* black forehead, wings and tail; canary-yellow body; wings show white in flight. *Female* and *Non-breeding male:* no black on forehead; yellow-green overall; gray-black wings and tail.
Size: 4¹/₂–5¹/₂ in.

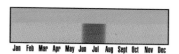

Jan Feb Mar Apr May Jun Jul Aug Sept Oct Nov Dec

Evening Grosbeak

Coccothraustes vespertinus

Unannounced, a flock of Evening Grosbeaks descends one chilly winter morning upon a feeder. For the proprietor of the feeder, the gold and black grosbeaks are both a blessing and a curse. The male's color is unmatched by other winter birds, and the social interaction in the flock is marvelous to watch, but the birds ravage sunflower stocks and send feeder operators outside daily to replenish the seed. Such incidents are not common even in the outskirts west of Denver, but the events are so noteworthy that, when they occur, stories circulate quickly through our birding community.

Evening Grosbeaks can be found at any time of year in our area, but they are most often seen from the end of the breeding season until spring. Like many other finches in the area, their numbers fluctuate from year to year, with booming years satisfying everyone's grosbeak needs. The Evening Grosbeak's trademark, large, conical bill is the most powerful bill per unit area of any bird in North America.

Similar Species: American Goldfinch (p. 138) is much smaller, and the black on its head is confined to the forehead.

Quick I.D.: smaller than a robin; large, conical bill. *Male:* yellow body; dark hood; black tail and wings; bold, white wing patches; yellow eyebrow stripe. *Female:* similar, but lacks bold eyebrow and bright gold body color.
Size: 7–8 in.

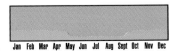

Jan Feb Mar Apr May Jun Jul Aug Sept Oct Nov Dec

Black-headed Grosbeak

Pheucticus melanocephalus

The male Black-headed Grosbeak has a brilliant voice to match his Halloween plumage, and he flaunts his song in treetop performances. This common songster's boldness does not go unnoticed by the appreciative birding community, which eagerly anticipates the male's annual spring concert. The female lacks the formal dress, but she shares her partner's musical talents. Whether the nest is tended by the male or female, the developing young are continually introduced into the world of song by the brooding parent.

This neotropical migrant nests in deciduous trees, such as those found in parts of Red Rocks Park or in less developed urban areas.

Similar Species: Spotted Towhee (p. 118) has a smaller bill and a longer tail. Female sparrows (pp. 117–27) are generally smaller.

Jan Feb Mar Apr May Jun Jul Aug Sept Oct Nov Dec

Quick I.D.: larger than a sparrow; light-colored, conical bill. *Male:* black head, wings and tail; orange body; white wing patches. *Female:* finely streaked with brown; white eyebrow; light throat.
Size: 7–8^1/$_2$ in.

Lazuli Bunting
Passerina amoena

♂

While hiking through the shrubby habitat of the Lazuli Bunting, one might soon notice the complexities of its songs. Neighboring males copy and learn from one another, producing 'song territories.' Each male within a song territory has personal variation to *swip-swip-swip zu zu ee, see see sip see see,* producing his own acoustic fingerprint.

Lazuli Buntings are widespread throughout our area during summer, popping out of dense bushes anywhere in Roxborough State Park. They build a small nest cup low to the ground in an upright crotch in a shrubby tangle. Once nesting duties are complete, these buntings are quick to leave our area, beginning their exodus in August after a partial molt.

These birds owe their name to the colorful gemstone lapis lazuli. The accepted pronunciation of the name is 'LAZZ-you-lie' (although most birders pronounce it 'LAZZ-oo-lee').

Similar Species: Western Bluebird is larger and lacks the wing bars. Indigo Bunting has no wing bars, and the male lacks the chestnut breast.

Quick I.D.: sparrow-sized. *Male:* turquoise blue hood and rump; chestnut breast; white belly; dark wings and tail; two white wing bars. *Female:* soft brown overall; hints of blue on rump.
Size: 5¹/₂ in.

Jan Feb Mar Apr May Jun Jul Aug Sept Oct Nov Dec

House Sparrow
Passer domesticus

This common backyard bird often confuses novice birdwatchers because females and immatures can be very nondescript. The male is relatively conspicuous— he has a black bib, a gray cap and white lines trailing down from his mouth (as though he has spilled milk on himself)—and he sings a continuous series of *cheep-cheep-cheep*s. The best field mark for the female, apart from her pale eyebrows, is the lack of distinctive field marks.

The House Sparrow was introduced to North America in the 1850s to control insects. Although this familiar bird can consume great quantities of insects, the majority of its diet is seeds, and it has become somewhat of a pest. The House Sparrow's aggressive nature usurps several native songbirds from nesting cavities, and its boldness often drives other birds away from backyard feeders. The House Sparrow and the European Starling, two of the most common birds in cities and on farms, are constant reminders of the negative impact of human introductions on natural systems.

Similar Species: Male is distinctive. Female is similar to unstreaked female sparrows (pp. 117–27) and female finches (pp. 135–38) but lacks any distinctive markings.

Quick I.D.: mid-sized sparrow; brownish-gray belly. *Male:* black throat; gray forehead; white jowls; chestnut nape. *Female:* unstreaked underparts; pale eyebrow; mottled wings and back.
Size: 5¹/₂–6¹/₂ in.

Jan Feb Mar Apr May Jun Jul Aug Sept Oct Nov Dec

Watching Birds

Identifying your first new bird can be so satisfying that you just might become addicted to birdwatching. Luckily, birdwatching does not have to be expensive. It all hinges on how involved in this hobby you want to get. Setting up a simple backyard feeder is an easy way to get to know the birds sharing your neighborhood, and some people simply find birdwatching a pleasant way to complement a nightly walk with the dog or a morning commute into work.

Many people enjoy going to urban parks and feeding the wild birds that have become accustomed to humans. This activity provides people with intimate contact with urban-dwelling birds, but remember that birdseed, or better yet the birds' natural food items, are much healthier for the birds than bread and crackers. As a spokesperson for the animals' health, kindly remind 'bread tossers' of the implications of their actions.

SEASONS OF BIRDWATCHING

Spring

Spring is probably the most favored season for birders, who welcome the arrival of the early migrants as much as the spring weather. By March, many birds of prey are already busy building their nests on the plains. When migrant land birds arrive March and April, it is still too early to ascend into the nearby foothills and mountains; they take shelter in the scattered forested areas of the lowlands until the frosty air warms.

In April, the tempo of bird migration escalates: many gulls, terns, sandpipers and other waterbirds descend on Denver's reservoirs, gathering in groups to rest and refuel before their northward journey continues. During May, the forested foothills and parks of Denver come alive with a bustling of activity. The Ruby-crowned Kinglet or Western Tanager can be heard singing in the canopy, and the distinctive foraging sounds of a Northern Flicker might attract birders to its whereabouts. Flocks of swallows grace the skies with their aerial acrobatics as many neotropical migrants make their long-awaited first appearance: the warblers and sparrows are among the last to filter through our area. Following their arrival and a few weeks of song battles, the pace of birdlife slows down—the task of nest building is at hand.

Summer

During the summer months, a transformation begins high in Denver's mountain parks. Up where the forest communities are reduced to sparse collections of stunted and twisted trees, the alpine and subalpine meadows become seas of wildflowers where hummingbirds sail. Meanwhile, at much lower elevations on the Great Plains, Swainson's and Ferruginous hawks, soaring on summer's thermals, are on their hunting vigil. In general, summertime finds birds busy with nesting duties. Once the chicks are born, the parents are kept busy feeding the insatiable young, and birders can occasionally witness the intriguing hunting behaviors of foraging birds.

Fall

The autumnal migrations begin in early August, with great flights of waterfowl traveling from the north to their wintering grounds. Many species common in the mountain parks prepare for their descent into the lower reaches of the foothills, and while the cottonwoods are changing color, the Say's Phoebe and Mountain Bluebird prepare for their departure from the grasslands around Denver.

An anticipated annual fall event is the passage of Swainson's Hawks through the Denver area on their way to Argentina. Many of the warblers, ducks, gulls and shorebirds have acquired frustratingly similar plumages during this season, but the fall migration has its own benefits: the movements of birds are not as concentrated as in spring, which provides a longer time frame for observing birds, and fall is also a good time for discovering rarities.

Winter

Winter is an unpredictable season in the Denver area. During warm and sunny periods, our local reservoirs will remain unfrozen and attract a variety of gulls, waterfowl and vigilant eagles. During prolonged cold snaps, however, these communities of birdlife diminish and the hardy winter birds concentrate in a few limited places.

Winter is a good time for watching your backyard feeder; finches, chickadees and juncos are common visitors to neighborhood yards. Many northern breeders are chased down into our area by the cold arctic air: Rough-legged Hawks, American Tree Sparrows and Horned Larks are regularly seen during Christmas bird counts—the highlight of many birders' calendars. If we are lucky, winter may even bring a fun rarity, such as the ever elusive Snowy Owl.

BIRDING OPTICS

Most people who are interested in birdwatching will eventually buy binoculars. They help you identify key bird characteristics, such as plumage and bill color, and they also help you identify other birders! Birdwatchers are a friendly sort, and a chat among birders is all part of the experience.

You'll use your binoculars often, so select a model that will contribute to the quality of your birdwatching experience—they don't have to be expensive. If you need help deciding which model is right for you, talk to other birdwatchers or to someone at your local nature center. Many models are available, and when shopping for binoculars it's important to keep two things in mind: weight and magnification.

One of the first things you'll notice about binoculars (apart from the price extremes) is that they all have two numbers associated with them (8x40, for example). The first number, which is always the smallest, is the magnification (how large the bird will appear), while the second is the size (in millimeters) of the objective lens (the larger end). It may seem important at first to get the highest magnification possible, but a reasonable magnification of 7x–8x is optimal for all-purpose birding, because it draws you fairly close to most birds without causing too much shaking. Some shaking happens to everyone; to overcome it, rest the binoculars against a support, such as a partner's shoulder or a tree.

The size of the objective lens is really a question of birding conditions and weight. Because wider lenses (40–50 mm) will bring in more light, these are preferred for birding in low-light situations (like before sunrise or after sunset). If these aren't the conditions that you will be pursuing, a light model that has an objective lens diameter of less than 30 mm may be the right choice. Because binoculars tend to become heavy after hanging around your neck all day, the compact models are becoming increasingly popular. If you have a model that is heavy, you can purchase a strap that redistributes part of the weight to the shoulders and lower back.

Another valuable piece of equipment is a spotting scope. It is very useful when you are trying to sight waterfowl, shorebirds or soaring raptors, but it is really of no use if you are intent on seeing forest birds. A good spotting scope has a magnification of around 40x. It has a sturdy tripod or a window mount for the car. Be wary of second-hand models of telescopes, as they are designed for seeing stars, and their magnifications are too great for birdwatching. One of the advantages of having a scope is that you will be able to see far-off birds, such as overwintering waterfowl and alcids on the ocean, or birds in migration, such as shorebirds and raptors. By setting up in one spot (or by not even leaving your car) you can observe faraway flocks that would be little more than specks in your binoculars.

With these simple pieces of equipment (none of which is truly essential) and this handy field guide, anyone can enjoy birds in their area. Many birds are difficult to see because they stay hidden in treetops, but you can learn to identify them by their songs. After experiencing the thrill of a couple of hard-won identifications, you will find yourself taking your binoculars on walks, drives and trips to the beach and cabin. As rewards accumulate with experience, you may find the books and photos piling up and your trips being planned just to see birds!

BIRDING BY EAR

Sometimes, bird listening can be more effective than bird watching. The technique of birding by ear is gaining popularity, because listening for birds can be more efficient, productive and rewarding than waiting for a visual confirmation. Birds have distinctive songs that they use to resolve territorial disputes, and sound is therefore a useful way to identify species. It is particularly useful when trying to watch some of the smaller forest-dwelling birds. Their size and often indistinct plumage can make a visual search of the forest canopy frustrating. To facilitate auditory searches, catchy paraphrases are included in the descriptions of many of the birds. If the paraphrase just doesn't seem to work for you (they are often a personal thing) be creative and try to find one that fits. By spending time playing the song over in your head, fitting words to it, the voices of birds soon become as familiar as the voices of family members. Many excellent CDs and tapes are available at bookstores and wild-bird stores for the songs of the birds in your area.

BIRDFEEDERS

They're messy, they can be costly, and they're sprouting up in neighborhoods everywhere. Feeding birds has become a common pastime in residential communities all over North America. Although the concept is fairly straightforward, as with anything else involving birds, feeders can become quite elaborate.

The great advantage to feeding birds is that neighborhood chickadees, jays, juncos and finches are enticed into regular visits. Don't expect birds to arrive at your feeder as soon as you set it up; it may take weeks for a few regulars to incorporate your yard into their daily routine. As the popularity of your feeder grows, the number of visiting birds will increase and more species will arrive. You will notice that your feeder is busier during the winter months, when natural foods are less abundant. You can increase the odds of a good avian turnout by using a variety of feeders and seeds. When a number of birds habitually visit your yard, maintaining the feeder becomes a responsibility, because the birds may begin to rely on it as a regular food source.

Larger birds tend to enjoy feeding on platforms or on the ground; smaller birds are comfortable on hanging seed dispensers. Certain seeds tend to attract specific birds; nature centers and wild-bird supply stores are the best places to ask how to attract a favorite species. It's mainly seed eaters that are attracted to backyards; some birds have no interest in feeders. Only the most committed birdwatcher will try to attract birds that are insect eaters, berry eaters or, in some extreme cases, scavengers!

The location of the feeder may influence the amount of business it receives from the neighborhood birds. Because birds are wild, they are instinctively wary, and they are unlikely to visit an area where they may come under attack. When putting up your feeder, think like a bird. A good, clear view with convenient escape routes is always appreciated. Cats like birdfeeders that are close to the ground and within pouncing distance from a bush; obviously, birds don't. Above all, a birdfeeder should be in view of a favorite window, where you can sit and enjoy the rewarding interaction of your appreciative feathered guests.

Glossary

accipiter: a forest hawk (genus Accipiter); characterized by a long tail and short, rounded wings; feeds mostly on birds.

brood: *n.* a family of young from one hatching; *v.* to sit on eggs so as to hatch them.

coniferous: cone-producing trees, usually softwood evergreens (e.g., spruce, pine, fir).

corvid: a member of the crow family (Corvidae); includes crows, jays, magpies and ravens.

covey: a brood or flock of partridges, quails or grouse.

crop: an enlargement of the esophagus, serving as a storage structure and (in pigeons) has glands which produce secretions.

dabbling: foraging technique used by ducks, where the head and neck are submerged but the body and tail remain on the water's surface.

dabbling duck: a duck that forages by dabbling; it can usually walk easily on land, it can take off without running, and it has a brightly colored speculum; includes Mallards, Gadwalls, teals and others.

deciduous: a tree that loses its leaves annually (e.g., oak, maple, aspen, birch).

dimorphism: the existence of two distinct forms of a species, such as between the sexes.

eclipse: the dull, female-like plumage that male ducks briefly acquire after molting from their breeding plumage.

elbow patches: dark spots at the bend of the outstretched wing, seen from below.

flycatching: feeding behavior where a bird leaves a perch, snatches an insect in mid-air, and returns to their previous perch; also known as 'hawking.'

fledgling: a young chick that has just acquired its permanent flight feathers, but is still dependent on its parents.

flushing: a behavior where frightened birds explode into flight in response to a disturbance.

gape: the size of the mouth opening.

irruption: a sporadic mass migration of birds into a non-breeding area.

larva: a development stage of an animal (usually an invertebrate) that has a different body form from the adult (e.g., caterpillar, maggot).

leading edge: the front edge of the wing as viewed from below.

litter: fallen plant material, such as twigs, leaves and needles, that forms a distinct layer above the soil, especially in forests.

lore: the small patch between the eye and the bill.

molting: the periodic replacement of worn out feathers (often twice a year).

morphology: the science of form and shape.

nape: the back of the neck.

neotropical migrant: a bird that nest in North America, but overwinters in the New World tropics.

niche: an ecological role filled by a species.

open country: a landscape that is primarily not forested.

parasitism: a relationship between two species where one benefits at the expense of the other.

phylogenetics: a method of classifying animals that puts the oldest ancestral groups before those that have arisen more recently.

pishing: making a sound to attract birds by saying pishhh as loudly and as wetly as comfortably possible.

polygynous: having a mating strategy where one male breeds with several females.

polyandrous: having a mating strategy where one female breeds with several males.

plucking post: a perch habitually used by an accipiter for plucking feathers from its prey.

raptor: a carnivorous (meat-eating) bird; includes eagles, hawks, falcons and owls.

rufous: rusty red in color.

speculum: a brightly colored patch in the wings of many dabbling ducks.

squeaking: making a sound to attract birds by loudly kissing the back of the hand, or by using a specially design squeaky bird call.

talons: the claws of birds of prey.

understorey: the shrub or thicket layer beneath a canopy of trees.

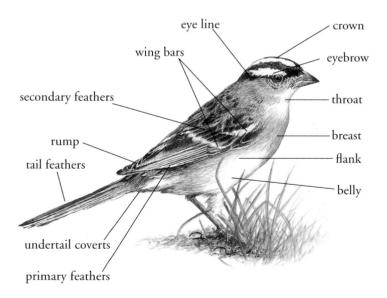

eye line

crown

wing bars

eyebrow

secondary feathers

throat

breast

rump

flank

tail feathers

belly

undertail coverts

primary feathers

References

American Ornithologists' Union. 1983–97. *Check-list of North American Birds.* 6th ed. (and its supplements). American Ornithologists' Union, Washington, D.C.

Andrews, R., and R. Righter. 1992. *Colorado Birds.* Denver Museum of Natural History, Denver.

Bailey, A.M., and R.J. Niedrach. 1965. *Birds of Colorado.* Denver Museum of Natural History, Denver.

Ehrlich, P.R., D.S. Dobkin and D. Wheye. 1988. *The Birder's Handbook.* Fireside, New York.

Evans, H.E. 1993. *Pioneer Naturalists: The Discovery and Naming of North American Plants and Animals.* Henry Holt and Co., New York.

Farrand, J., ed. 1983. *The Audubon Society Master Guide to Birding.* Vols. 1–3. Alfred A. Knopf, New York.

Folzenlogen, R. 1995. *Birding the Front Range.* Willow Press, Littleton, Colorado.

Gotch, A.F. 1981. *Birds: Their Latin Names Explained.* Blandford Press, Dorset, England.

Holt, H.R. 1997. *A Birder's Guide to Colorado.* American Birding Association, Colorado Springs.

Mearns, B., and R. Mearns. 1992. *Audubon to Xantus: The Lives of Those Commemorated in North American Bird Names.* Academic Press, San Diego.

National Audubon Society. 1971–95. *American Birds.* Vols. 25–48.

Peterson, R.T. 1990. *A Field Guide to the Western Birds.* 3rd ed. Houghton Mifflin Co., Boston.

Reader's Digest Association. *Book of North American Birds.* The Reader's Digest Association, Pleasantville, New York.

Robbins, C.S., B. Brunn and H.S. Zim. 1966. *Birds of North America.* Golden Press, New York.

Scott, S.S. 1987. *Field Guide to the Birds of North America.* National Geographic Society, Washington, D.C.

Stokes, D., and L. Stokes. 1996. *Stokes Field Guide to Birds: Western Region.* Little, Brown and Co., Boston.

Terres, J.K. 1995. *The Audubon Society Encyclopedia of North American Birds.* Wings Books, New York.

Checklist of Denver-area Birds

This checklist includes a total of 294 bird species recorded in Denver and the surrounding foothills and front range. It was compiled using the Denver Field Ornithologists' field trip report form (1995) and *Birds of Colorado* (Andrews and Righter 1992).

Checklist symbols:

Seasons

W = Winter (mid-December through February)
Sp = Spring (March through early June)
Su = Summer (mid-July through July)
F = Fall (August through December)

Breeding Status

B = Regular breeder (nests every year)
b = Irregular breeder (nests infrequently; few nesting records)
? = Suspected breeder (no confirmation of nesting)
+ = Former breeder (no nesting records in recent years)
L = Local breeder (restricted to a few locations)

Abundance

(in appropriate habitats)

C = Common to abundant (always present in large numbers)
F = Fairly common (always present in moderate to small numbers)
U = Uncommon (usually present in small numbers)
R = Rare (observed in very small numbers, and perhaps not every year)
X = Extremely rare (fewer than 10 recorded sightings during that season)
- = Absent (no recorded sightings)
e = Erratic (can occur in substantially larger or smaller numbers during certain years)
* = Abundance in high mountains west of Denver

The species in this checklist are listed in taxonomic order (in accordance with the 41st supplement [July 1997] of the American Ornithologists' Union's *Check-list of North American Birds*). A blank line separates each family of birds. This checklist does not include 'accidental' species (recorded fewer than 10 times ever in our area).

	W	Sp	Su	F
Pacific Loon	-	-	-	R
Common Loon	R	U	R	U
Pied-billed Grebe (B)	R	F	F	F
Horned Grebe	R	F	X	F
Red-necked Grebe	-	R	-	R
Eared Grebe	X	C	U	C
Western Grebe (B)	R	C	C	C
Clark's Grebe (B)	X	U	U	U
American White Pelican	-	C	C	C
Double-crested Cormorant (B)	R	C	C	C
American Bittern (B)	X	U	U	U
Least Bittern (BL)	-	R	R	R
Great Blue Heron (B)	R	C	C	C
Great Egret (BL)	-	R	R	R
Snowy Egret (b)	-	R	R	R
Little Blue Heron	-	X	X	X
Cattle Egret (BL)	-	R	U	R
Green Heron	-	R	R	R
Black-crowned Night-Heron (B)	R	U	U	U
Yellow-crowned Night-Heron (+)	-	X	X	X
White-faced Ibis	-	U	X	R
Turkey Vulture	-	U	R	U
Greater White-fronted Goose	R	R	-	R
Snow Goose	R	F	-	F
Ross's Goose	R	R	-	X
Canada Goose (B)	C	C	F	C
Tundra Swan	X	R	-	R
Wood Duck (BL)	R	R	R	R
Gadwall (B)	R	C	U	C
American Wigeon (B)	U	C	U	C
Mallard (B)	C	C	C	C
Blue-winged Teal (B)	X	C	C	C
Cinnamon Teal (B)	R	C	C	C
Northern Shoveler (B)	R	C	U	C
Northern Pintail (B)	U	C	U	C
Green-winged Teal (B)	R	C	R	C
Canvasback (+)	R	U	X	U

	W	Sp	Su	F
Redhead (B)	R	C	U	C
Ring-necked Duck	R	U	U	U
Greater Scaup	R	R	-	R
Lesser Scaup (+)	U	C	U	C
Surf Scoter	X	-	-	R
White-winged Scoter	X	-	-	R
Oldsquaw	X	-	-	R
Bufflehead	U	F	X	F
Common Goldeneye	C	C	X	C
Barrow's Goldeneye	R	R	-	R
Hooded Merganser	R	R	X	R
Red-breasted Merganser	R	U	-	U
Common Merganser (BL)	C	C	R	C
Ruddy Duck (B)	R	C	R	C
Osprey	-	U	-	R
Bald Eagle (BL)	U	R	R	R
Northern Harrier (B)	U	U	R	U
Sharp-shinned Hawk	U	U	R	U
Cooper's Hawk	R	U	R	U
Northern Goshawk	U	U	R	U
Broad-winged Hawk	-	R	-	X
Swainson's Hawk (B)	-	F	F	F
Red-tailed Hawk (B)	F	F	U	F
Ferruginous Hawk	U	R	R	R
Rough-legged Hawk	U	R	-	R
Golden Eagle (BL)	U	R	R	R
American Kestrel (B)	U	C	U	C
Merlin	R	R	-	R
Prairie Falcon (BL)	U	R	R	R
Peregrine Falcon (BL)	X	R	R	R
Ring-necked Pheasant (B)	F	F	F	F
Blue Grouse	U	U	U	U
White-tailed Ptarmigan	R*	R*	R*	R*
Wild Turkey (B)	R	R	R	R
Northern Bobwhite	R	R	R	R
Virginia Rail (B)	R	U	U	U
Sora (B)	X	U	U	U
American Coot (B)	U	C	F	C
Sandhill Crane	-	R	-	U
Black-bellied Plover	-	R	-	U

	W	Sp	Su	F
American Golden-Plover .. -	X	-		R
Snowy Plover ... -	X	-		X
Semipalmated Plover ... -	R	-		U
Killdeer (B) .... R	C	F		C
Mountain Plover (+) ... -	U	U		U
Black-necked Stilt (BL) ..... -	R	X		R
American Avocet (B) ... -	C	U		C
Greater Yellowlegs ... -	U	R		U
Lesser Yellowlegs ... -	F	R		C
Solitary Sandpiper ... -	U	R		U
Willet ... -	U	R		R
Spotted Sandpiper (B) ... -	F	U		F
Long-billed Curlew (+) ... -	R	R		R
Marbled Godwit ... -	R	X		R
Red Knot ... -	X	-		R
Sanderling ... -	R	-		R
Semipalmated Sandpiper .. -	R	-		U
Western Sandpiper ... -	R	R		U
Least Sandpiper ... -	R	R		U
Baird's Sandpiper ... -	R	R		C
Pectoral Sandpiper ... -	R	-		U
Stilt Sandpiper ... -	R	X		U
Long-billed Dowitcher ... -	U	R		F
Common Snipe (B) ... U	F	U		F
Wilson's Phalarope ... -	C	R		F
Red-necked Phalarope ... -	U	X		U
Franklin's Gull ... -	F	R		C
Bonaparte's Gull ... -	U	-		U
Ring-billed Gull ... C	C	F		C
California Gull ... R	C	U		C
Herring Gull ... C	R	-		R
Thayer's Gull ... R	-	-		-
Glaucous Gull ... R	-	-		-
Sabine's Gull ... -	-	-		R
Common Tern ... -	R	X		U
Forster's Tern ... -	U	R		U
Black Tern ... -	C	R		U
Rock Dove (B) ... C	C	C		C
Band-tailed Pigeon ... -	U	U		U
Mourning Dove (B) ... U	C	C		C
Yellow-billed Cuckoo ... -	-	R		R
Black-billed Cuckoo ... -	-	X		-

	W	Sp	Su	F
Barn Owl (B) ...	X	R	R	R
Flammulated Owl ... -	R	R	R	
Eastern Screech-Owl (B) ... U	U	U	U	
Great Horned Owl (B) ... U	U	U	U	
Snowy Owl ... Re	-	-	-	
Northern Pygmy-Owl ... R	R	R	R	
Burrowing Owl (B) ... -	U	U	U	
Long-eared Owl (BL) ... R	R	R	R	
Short-eared Owl (BL) ... Re	Re	X	X	
Northern Saw-whet Owl ... U	U	U	U	
Common Nighthawk (B) ... -	U	F	F	
Common Poorwill (B) ... -	U	U	U	
Chimney Swift (B) ... -	U	U	U	
White-throated Swift ... -	C	C	C	
Broad-tailed Hummingbird (B) ... -	F	F	F	
Calliope Hummingbird ... -	-	R	R	
Rufous Hummingbird ... -	-	U	U	
Belted Kingfisher ... R	U	U	U	
Lewis's Woodpecker ... X	R	X	R	
Red-headed Woodpecker (B) ... -	R	R	R	
Red-naped Sapsucker ... -	U	U	U	
Williamson's Sapsucker ... -	U	U	U	
Downy Woodpecker (B) ... F	F	U	F	
Hairy Woodpecker (B) ... U	U	U	U	
Northern Flicker (B) ... C	C	C	C	
Olive-sided Flycatcher ... -	U	U*	U	
Western Wood-Pewee ... -	F	F	F	
Willow Flycatcher (B) ... -	U	U	U	
Least Flycatcher ... -	R	X	R	
Hammond's Flycatcher (BL) ... -	R	R	R	
Dusky Flycatcher (B) ... -	U	U	-	
Cordilleran Flycatcher (B) ... -	U	U	U	
Eastern Phoebe ... -	R	-	R	
Say's Phoebe (B) ... -	U	U	U	
Ash-throated Flycatcher ... -	R	-	R	

	W	Sp	Su	F
❏ Great Crested Flycatcher	-	R	-	R
❏ Cassin's Kingbird	-	R	-	R
❏ Western Kingbird (B)	-	U	C	U
❏ Eastern Kingbird (B)	-	U	C	U
❏ Northern Shrike	U	X	-	X
❏ Loggerhead Shrike (B)	R	U	U	U
❏ Plumbeous Vireo (B)	-	F	F	F
❏ Warbling Vireo (B)	-	U	U	U
❏ Red-eyed Vireo (BL)	-	U	R	U
❏ Gray Jay	R	R	R	R
❏ Steller's Jay (B)	F	F	F	F
❏ Blue Jay (B)	U	U	U	F
❏ Western Scrub-Jay	U	U	U	U
❏ Pinyon Jay	Re	-	-	Re
❏ Clark's Nutcracker	Re	R	R	R
❏ Black-billed Magpie (B)	C	C	C	C
❏ American Crow (B)	C	F	F	C
❏ Common Raven (B)	U	U	U	U
❏ Horned Lark (B)	R	U	R	U
❏ Tree Swallow (B)	-	F	F	F
❏ Violet-green Swallow (B)	-	U	U	U
❏ Northern Rough-winged Swallow (B)	-	F	U	U
❏ Bank Swallow (B)	-	U	U	U
❏ Barn Swallow (B)	-	C	C	C
❏ Cliff Swallow (B)	-	C	C	C
❏ Black-capped Chickadee (B)	F	F	F	F
❏ Mountain Chickadee (B)	Fe	Fe	Fe	Fe
❏ Bushtit	R	X	X	X
❏ Red-breasted Nuthatch (b)	Re	Fe	X	Fe
❏ White-breasted Nuthatch (B)	R	U	R	U
❏ Pygmy Nuthatch (B)	F	F	F	F
❏ Brown Creeper	U	U	-	U
❏ Rock Wren	X	U	U	U

	W	Sp	Su	F
❏ Canyon Wren	U	U	U	U
❏ House Wren (B)	-	F	F	F
❏ Winter Wren	R	-	-	-
❏ Marsh Wren (BL)	R	R	R	R
❏ American Dipper (B)	F	F	F	F
❏ Golden-crowned Kinglet	U	U	U*	U
❏ Ruby-crowned Kinglet (B)	X	F	F	F
❏ Blue-gray Gnatcatcher	-	U	-	U
❏ Eastern Bluebird (BL)	X	R	X	R
❏ Western Bluebird	R	R	R	R
❏ Mountain Bluebird (+)	U	F	U	F
❏ Townsend's Solitaire (B)	U	U	U	U
❏ Veery (B)	-	R	R	X
❏ Swainson's Thrush (B)	-	F	R	F
❏ Hermit Thrush (B)	X	F	F	F
❏ American Robin (B)	C	C	C	C
❏ European Starling (B)	C	C	C	C
❏ Gray Catbird (B)	-	U	U	U
❏ Northern Mockingbird (B)	X	R	R	R
❏ Sage Thrasher (B)	X	U	R	U
❏ Brown Thrasher (BL)	X	U	R	U
❏ American Pipit	U	F	F*	F
❏ Bohemian Waxwing	Ce	Re	-	-
❏ Cedar Waxwing (B)	Ue	Ue	Re	Ue
❏ Tennessee Warbler	-	R	-	R
❏ Orange-crowned Warbler	-	F	R	F
❏ Nashville Warbler	-	R	-	R
❏ Virginia's Warbler (B)	-	U	U	U
❏ Northern Parula	-	R	-	X
❏ Yellow Warbler (B)	-	C	C	C
❏ Chestnut-sided Warbler (BL)	-	R	R	X
❏ Magnolia Warbler	-	R	-	R
❏ Black-throated Blue Warbler	-	R	-	R
❏ Yellow-rumped Warbler	R	C	F*	C

	W	Sp	Su	F
❑ Black-throated Gray Warbler	-	R	-	R
❑ Townsend's Warbler	-	-	-	R
❑ Black-throated Green Warbler	-	R	-	R
❑ Blackburnian Warbler	-	R	-	X
❑ Palm Warbler	-	R	-	R
❑ Bay-breasted Warbler	-	R	-	-
❑ Blackpoll Warbler	-	R	-	-
❑ Black-and-white Warbler	-	R	-	R
❑ American Redstart (BL)	-	U	R	U
❑ Worm-eating Warbler	-	R	-	R
❑ Ovenbird (B)	-	R	R	R
❑ Northern Waterthrush	-	R	-	R
❑ MacGillivray's Warbler (B)	-	U	U	U
❑ Common Yellowthroat (B)	-	C	C	C
❑ Hooded Warbler	-	R	-	-
❑ Wilson's Warbler	-	U	F*	C
❑ Yellow-breasted Chat (BL)	-	U	F	U
❑ Summer Tanager	-	R	-	R
❑ Western Tanager (B)	-	F	F	F
❑ Green-tailed Towhee (B)	X	F	F	F
❑ Spotted Towhee (B)	R	U	R	U
❑ Cassin's Sparrow	-	R	R	R
❑ American Tree Sparrow	C	U	-	U
❑ Chipping Sparrow (B)	X	C	C	C
❑ Clay-colored Sparrow	-	U	-	U
❑ Brewer's Sparrow (B)	-	F	U	F
❑ Field Sparrow	-	R	-	R
❑ Vesper Sparrow (B)	-	C	C	C
❑ Lark Sparrow (B)	-	F	F	F
❑ Lark Bunting (B)	X	U	U	U
❑ Savannah Sparrow (B)	-	C	U	C
❑ Grasshopper Sparrow (BL)	-	Re	Re	Re
❑ Song Sparrow (B)	C	C	F	C
❑ Lincoln's Sparrow	-	U	F*	U
❑ Swamp Sparrow	R	R	-	R
❑ White-throated Sparrow	R	R	-	U
❑ Harris's Sparrow	U	U	-	U

	W	Sp	Su	F
❑ White-crowned Sparrow	C	C	-	C
❑ Dark-eyed Junco (B)	C	C	C	C
❑ McCown's Longspur	-	R	-	R
❑ Lapland Longspur	Re	R	-	Re
❑ Chestnut-collared Longspur	-	R	-	R
❑ Snow Bunting	Re	-	-	-
❑ Northern Cardinal	R	R	R	R
❑ Rose-breasted Grosbeak	-	R	R	R
❑ Black-headed Grosbeak (B)	-	U	R	U
❑ Blue Grosbeak (B)	-	U	U	U
❑ Lazuli Bunting (B)	-	U	U	U
❑ Indigo Bunting (B)	-	R	R	R
❑ Dickcissel (b)	-	Re	Re	Re
❑ Bobolink (BL)	-	R	R	R
❑ Red-winged Blackbird (B)	C	C	C	C
❑ Western Meadowlark (B)	C	C	C	C
❑ Yellow-headed Blackbird (B)	R	C	C	C
❑ Rusty Blackbird	R	X	-	R
❑ Brewer's Blackbird	U	U	U	U
❑ Common Grackle (B)	R	C	C	C
❑ Brown-headed Cowbird (B)	R	C	C	F
❑ Orchard Oriole (BL)	-	R	R	-
❑ Bullock's Oriole (B)	X	C	C	U
❑ Gray-crowned Rosy-Finch	Fe	-	-	-
❑ Black Rosy-Finch	Re	-	-	-
❑ Brown-capped Rosy-Finch	Ue	U*	U*	U*
❑ Pine Grosbeak	Re	R*	R*	Re
❑ Cassin's Finch	Fe	F*	F*	F*
❑ House Finch (B)	C	C	C	C
❑ Red Crossbill	Fe	Fe	Fe	Fe
❑ Common Redpoll	Fe	-	-	-
❑ Pine Siskin	Ue	Ue	U*	Ue
❑ Lesser Goldfinch	-	R	R	R
❑ American Goldfinch (B)	F	C	U	C
❑ Evening Grosbeak (b)	Fe	Fe	Re	Fe
❑ House Sparrow (B)	C	C	C	C

Index of Scientific Names

This index references only the primary, illustrated species descriptions.

Index of Common Names

Boldface page numbers refer to the primary, illustrated species descriptions.

About the Authors

When he's not out watching birds, frogs or snakes, Chris Fisher researches endangered species management and wildlife interpretation in the Department of Renewable Resources at the University of Alberta. The appeal of western wildlife and wilderness has led to many travels, including frequent visits with birds. Chris's first city bird guide was *Birds of Seattle*, and since then he has co-authored similar books for San Francisco, Los Angeles and San Diego. Now he has his binoculars focused on other cities. By sharing his enthusiasm and passion for wild things through lectures, photographs and articles, Chris strives to foster a greater appreciation for the value of our wilderness.

Greg Butcher brings to this project a lifetime of birding experience from across America (all 49 continental states, Canada, Belize, Costa Rica and Panama). He has been the executive director of the American Birding Association since 1993, and before that he was director of Bird Population Studies at the Cornell Laboratory of Ornithology (from 1984 to 1993). Greg began birding at the age of 11, after visiting his grandfather in Carmel, California; he's added at least one bird to his life list every year since. He studied zoology at both Connecticut College (B.A.) and the University of Washington (Ph.D.). He is a past president of the Association of Field Ornithologists and chair of the Nongovernmental Organizations Committee of Partners in Flight, the neotropical migratory bird conservation program. Greg makes his home in Colorado Springs.

This easy-to-use and beautifully illustrated guidebook will help you identify the feathered strangers nibbling at the feeder in your backyard or singing from a nearby tree. It's packed with notes on 125 common and interesting bird species in and around Denver:

❖ easy identification
❖ songs and calls
❖ habitat, nests and food
❖ similar species
❖ a checklist to help you keep track of your birdwatching experiences
❖ birdfeeders for your yard
❖ tips on the best birding spots in our area.

$9.95

Whether you're a beginner birder or an amateur naturalist, you will find *Birds of Denver and the Front Range* a handy reference for our parks, backyards and natural areas.